Marketing
Plus

*A positive approach to total
management*

David Joseph and
Tony McBurnie

Heinemann Professional Publishing

Heinemann Professional Publishing Ltd
Halley Court, Jordan Hill, Oxford OX2 8EJ

OXFORD   LONDON   MELBOURNE   AUCKLAND   SINGAPORE
IBADAN   NAIROBI   GABORONE   KINGSTON

First published by Heinemann Publishers New Zealand 1987
First published in Great Britain by Heinemann Professional Publishing Ltd 1989

British Library Cataloguing in Publication Data

Joseph, David
    Marketing plus.
    1. Marketing. Manuals
    I. Title   II. McBurnie, Tony.
    658.8.

ISBN 0 434 90908 4

Photoset by Deltatype Ltd, Ellesmere Port
Printed by Unwin Brothers Ltd.,
The Gresham Press, Old Woking, Surrey GU22 9LH
A Member of the Martins Printing Group

Contents

Preface

This book is not an academic treatise. It is a practical collection of 'essays' that aims to examine marketing philosophy, to explain marketing in simple language, and to provide guidelines and applications pertinent to a wide cross-section of businesses.

Much of the content is based on published articles, broadcasts, lectures and seminar notes prepared by the authors over the past decade. Additionally, international management experience, extensive project work, research and consulting for a variety of companies and organisations have provided a platform from which many of the guidelines have been drawn.

The marketing label is in many respects too narrow to summarise this book's purpose. By its very nature, the modern marketing craft is a *total* management approach that affects all aspects of a business. Marketing must never be looked at in isolation – this is why we have explored other business functions and activities.

Marketing Plus: A positive approach to total management is designed to provide practical help to business people (or for that matter anyone seeking a better understanding of what marketing is about). Readers may be connected with a large or small organisation; they may be self-employed and wondering whether marketing is affordable or necessary; they may be providing goods or services; their markets may comprise consumers or industrial buyers. Whichever profile fits, the goal is to help you gain an uncluttered, simplified, improved and relevant understanding of how the marketing perception can help your specific activities.

Finally, we do not pretend that the ideas or guidelines expressed here are revolutionary. There is very little around in the way of new ideas. Rather, the intention is to provide improved approaches to solving old problems. Consequently, if the use of *Marketing Plus: A positive approach to total management* sparks one new idea for an individual reader; if it encourages a thought or question designed to aid improvement; if it forces you to look critically at your business activities and ask 'What am I doing? How well am I doing it?' – then the exercise has been worthwhile.

1

What is marketing?

Marketing is very much misunderstood. There still remains in many quarters an incorrect belief that marketing is a fancy word for selling or advertising. However, real marketing affects our lives daily as consumers, manufacturers of goods, or providers of services. It also influences corporate success or failure, and effective marketing stimulates industrial output, creates jobs and enhances national prosperity.

The days of paying lip service to marketing have gone; no longer is it good enough to change a sales manager's title to 'marketing manager', or to proclaim that because you have displayed some streak of entrepreneurial flair, you are 'into marketing'.

Marketing is, above all else, concerned with customers and the competition for their choice. Sometimes the customers are readily identified, more often you have to look for them and find where they are hidden. Similarly competitors are often obvious, but in many cases the indirect competition can be more of a threat to your business. Thus there is a need for a far more professional attitude to marketing.

In some smaller companies and indeed in some smaller countries, there is also a view that professional marketing is only for those connected with the movement of consumer goods, large organisations with major national or international brands. Nothing could be further from the truth.

Marketing is necessary because customers have a choice and you need to convince them that they should buy your product or service, rather than those on offer from competitors. In most countries the vast majority of businesses are small- or medium-sized, and in most countries the major reason for business failure is not a poor product or service, but a lack of understanding of customers, and how to beat the competition for those customers.

Irrespective of the size or nature of your business, the increased sophistication required to trade successfully and profitably, coupled with local and foreign competitors, dictates that you must pay regard to the basic marketing truism.

In any competitive situation, the organisation which really knows its markets, its customers, their problems and their needs, has the best chance of producing and presenting the product or service they will want to buy, and thereby exposes itself to the risk of making profit.

This in turn means that you must:

- Plan your marketing in a formal manner.
- Constantly measure and examine the results of your marketing effort.
- Be prepared to adapt your marketing approach to suit the changes dictated by, among other things, a fickle market place, direct and indirect competition, the cost of money, new technology and lifestyles.

Marketing definitions abound. They range from 'identifying opportunities', 'a movement from concept through to consumer', 'product, place, price, promotion' and 'satisfying needs', through to 'something the Americans invented along with Coke'. One very succinct summation comes from the Institute of Marketing in the UK: 'the management function responsible for identifying, anticipating and satisfying customers' requirements profitably'. Profitably needs to be emphasised, because far too many people do not include that key word. After all, if there is no profit you may as well walk away from your enterprise. This additional focus on profit is also a reminder that marketing has an impact on many aspects of business, for until a customer buys there is no business.

The reality of marketing

Marketing is quite simply the child of competition and customer choice. It is only necessary because customers need a reason for preferring one product or service to another. It has two elements:
- An acceptance that until the customer buys, you are not in business – the supremacy of the customer.
- A set of disciplines and activities for influencing customers to buy your offering in preference to competitors.

The main activities are the following.

Research

It is essential to find out as much as possible about markets, products or services. Research need not be expensive. Much of it can be carried out by utilising your own resources, and making the most of published data and free information sources.

Properly introduced, research takes the guesswork out of predictions related to customers, products and territories. Moreover, it should be used to monitor the effects and accuracy of the other elements in the marketing mix. Research *is not* a stop/start affair.

Development

This covers new and improved products and services; territories, diversifications; additions and deletions.

Pricing

Self-explanatory: you must ensure that you are competitive and profitable, heeding special circumstances such as volume, repeat business or marginal criteria, competition and opportunity.

Selling

This must embody specialist skills, advisory services and technical excellence. With rising costs for salaries, vehicles etc., selling calls for new methods: analysing customers, defining justified levels of service, and classifying the frequency and type of contact (whether face to face, by telephone, or by letter).

Advertising and promotion

Along with public relations, this is an emotive area. It extends into a plethora of subelements, which can include point-of-sale material, merchandising aids, packaging design, presentation and so on.

Maintain perspective by thinking about this element in terms of *communication*. A can of baked beans is communicating something via a label, name, television advertisement or whatever. Its message may be taste, value for money, good nutrition, or easy preparation.

Insufficient attention is often given to the role that communication must play. Many essential aspects are all too frequently overlooked – heaven knows how much money is frittered away on senseless, poorly planned advertising. Ask yourself what image you need to project, and ensure that your message or invitation encourages action.

Identify your assorted audiences. Basically, a company's market can be subdivided into a *number* of publics. Each public may well respond to different messages or platforms. Intermediaries, be they stockists, distributors or referral sources, are aroused by communication technique and content, which, in turn, can influence the supplier's success or failure. An engineer will not give a hoot for the 'new improved, whiter than white' type of promise that encourages the supermarket shopper to draw a bead on a brand leader's shelf space.

To sound one further warning: remember that communication needs to be beamed inside as well as outside an organisation. In other words, those publics we refer to include your own people. They, too, must believe in your product or service. They, too, must be communicated to in an efficient, motivating manner.

Distribution

This involves scrutinising the movement of a product or service from your base to buying points. It is important to check whether you should be controlling distribution via your own resources or whether the utilisation of funds might be improved by relying more upon intermediaries such as agents or distributors.

Distribution reviews must also monitor transport methods, warehousing and inventory control, where applicable.

Service and after-sales service

Like profitability in our definition of marketing, service and after-sales service are essential to foster good business. Yet they tend to be neglected.

Closing the sale and obtaining the order – that is important. At the same time, if repeat business is the aim then look closely at follow-up deliveries, quality control, transportation and other service aspects.

Marketing sense ensures survival

As competition and the struggle to gain buyers' attention increases, businesses will divide into two camps – the quick and the dead. Those who still think that marketing is only selling with a fancy label hung round its neck will be among the commercially dead.

Peter Drucker, the eminent professor of management and highly respected business author, talks about 'sloughing off yesterday' and the need to 'feed opportunities, starve problems'. Yesterday's solutions have a bearing, but they may require comprehensive adaptation and checking to satisfy today's real needs.

Improvement may be emerging, but we still witness too much preoccupation with product orientation. Survival and growth means learning to be market oriented. The orientation cycle gets under way with an approach that asks:

- What does or will the market need?
- Can we produce to satisfy that need?
- Will it be profitable to us?

So, above all else, adopt a questioning approach to business – one that does not take your customers or your markets for granted; one that forces you to double-check your activities rather than shrug and say, 'We've always done it this way'.

This change in emphasis has been emerging for several decades. Unfortunately, however, some of us are slower than others when it comes to comprehending change and its dictates.

Between the First World War and the Second World War (and after the latter), the design and use of products changed slowly. Businesses concentrated on increased productions; shortages abounded. Remember the waiting lists for new cars, with dealers offering murderous trade-in allowances (and insisting on a trade-in), then informing you of a three-month wait, and finally telling you, 'It comes in blue – take it or leave it.' Quick cut to the 1980s: the same dealer offers free trips, appliances, cash deals, bonus extras, easy payment terms . . . and no trade-in is required.

This illustrates a change in emphasis: supply now exceeds demand. As this turnaround emerged, suppliers moved from product or production orientation to sales orientation – 'We're making these things; get out there and sell them'. An eager market, hungry for consumer luxuries, kept the production lines rolling.

Now there's a new ball game, with no prizes for coming second. We talk about market orientation – providing what the *customer* wants. The wheel has turned: from selling just about all one could supply – one might say a management of shortages – to having to push goods (or services) out. In other words, today's trading climate means a management of surpluses.

And there's more to this new direction than meets the eye. Technological advances, increased competition for a slice of the spender's cake, global competition – these are some of the challenges faced by marketers.

The customer comes first

Customers' needs are of paramount importance. Compare today's customer or buyer with his or her counterpart of, say 20 or 30 years ago. What do we find? Our prime prospect is a shrewd, calculating decision-maker. Today, people are better educated; they are less susceptible to false claims; they will rarely buy a poor product twice (and, for most of us, repeat business is what we are after). Discerning housewives and laid-back teenagers shop around. They compare the variety of offers before deciding which and where to purchase.

Bread-winners and household heads have been forced to be more careful about how they spend their disposable income. The same can be said for companies – cash flow, husbanding of purchasing allocations, settlement terms – smart corporate buyers seek an extra edge to contribute to an improved bottom line.

This era of change, which governs the up/down business environment, means more brand switching and less loyalty. There is a wide selection of goodies and suppliers to choose from. We all tend to shop around – not only for our staples but also for our non-day-to-day requirements. 'Shopping around' covers banks, insurance companies, professional advisers, doctors and so on. The 'womb-to-tomb/we have always done business with them' mentality is dying fast.

Back to basics

For many, the path to survival and expansion means a return to basics. Now this, in some ways, may sound like a contradiction in terms. Here we are, advocating the application of a management tool, discipline, craft . . . call it what you will, and in the next gasp we are advocating a return to basics.

'Basics' in this context means checking what business we are in. Where do our real (not imagined) opportunities lie? What are we actually selling – what benefits do our products or services provide to our customers?

Face up to your operation's weaknesses as well as its strengths. Ascertain the threats to your business, your customers, your markets. Then get on with the job of devising solutions. Once the problem is defined, you are half-way towards finding an answer. Do not ever confuse problems with troubles. Many a business has traded from the red into the black and turned adversity into success by capitalising on hidden opportunities – opportunities that have only surfaced thanks to a critical look at faults and threats. Remember that a problem is simply an opportunity in disguise.

When defining the benefits you provide, set them down in terms of how they affect the end-user. You may have heard it before, but it is still worth repeating: features are what the product or service incorporates; benefits are what motivate the buyer/user. So the manufacturers of electric drills are selling holes; the makers of cosmetics are selling hope; the IBMs of this world are selling organised systems and efficiency.

Define what you are *really* selling. Perhaps you are selling savings – saving people time, money, effort or whatever. You must be able to define exactly what business you are really in. Concentrate on being superb at which you do best, instead of trying to be all things to all customers. Resist the temptation to rush off in new directions. Rather, target your efforts so that you improve internal cost efficiency, systems and productivity, as well as placing yourself in a situation allowing external price efficiency.

During tough (or competitive) trading times, it is important to avoid a negative outlook. Elements of the media and the Government frequently foster such tendencies, sensationalism and gloom being the orders of the day.

The disposable income is still there, but the customers are more discerning – from the housewife trying to stretch her food budget, to the purchasing officer deciding which high-cost capital item will prove the best investment.

Research has proven that price, though a factor, is frequently outweighed by quality, service and other influencing factors.

Marketing must make us constantly aware of the high cost of money. The rougher, tougher trading climate means that you have to keep a closer watch on your bottom line – from collection ratios to risk exposure. You also need to keep constantly attuned to your markets and customers. Marketing planning and financial planning go hand in hand.

It is worth adding a cautionary note at this point: beware of false prophets. Chartered accountants, lawyers, bankers and the like are essential allies and advisers. Unfortunately – and it may have something to do with the relative 'newness' of the marketing craft – such people feel that they are qualified to advise on trading and marketing, when, in fact some would not know an export incentive from a suspensory loan.

Interaction is vital

Understanding means that each management sphere must appreciate its fellow functions. Conflict often surfaces between sections. Many self-styled marketers cannot abide financial accountants, with the result that, in time, each becomes anathema to the other.

This same sparring can occur between marketing and production, or marketing and personnel. But the problem should not exist when one considers that a determination to understand the other parties' requirements, is supposed to be the basic tenet of marketing.

The example of accountants versus marketers is highlighted because the bloodiest boardroom confrontations seem to arise between these two groups. This was summed up well by a sales executive who once commented, 'Sales and production hate one another's guts, but the common enemy is accounts.'

And yet these two 'enemies' – in fact all the 'parts' of management – must work in harmony to create a better 'whole'.

Understanding is the key to peaceful co-existence – understanding each other's sphere, and educating your sectional colleagues on what you do and why you do it.

The ability to analyse and grasp the meaning of figures is a prerequisite in marketing. Getting to grips with what is behind the figures relating to profit, product emphasis, waste, raw materials, and so on is imperative. Accountants will themselves tell you that a balance sheet is little more than a photograph of a company at a particular point in time. Mind you, some marketers would embellish that by claiming that the same balance sheet comprises two columns of lies adding up to the same figure!

In the end, getting to grips with the figures, trends and extrapolations becomes crucial. Our marketing definition involves *anticipation*. It is essential to read the signs in advance, stay alert, and be ready to capitalise on opportunities or adjust your tactics to combat threats.

Using anticipation to satisfy needs or opportunities leads us into the specific use of a variety of tools – a marketing mix. The elements are many and varied, and we will be examining each in subsequent chapters.

Examples

The lack of marketing understanding has been evident in many industries and was highlighted by Ted Levitt in his famous *Marketing Myopia* article. He shocked US management by maintaining that companies often failed because they did not understand the markets or business they were in. Hollywood considered it was in movies and was almost destroyed by television before it realised it was in the entertainment business.

The railroad companies let road transport and airline competitors take their business, because they did not see their markets as passenger and freight transportation.

The motorcycle industry in the UK virtually disappeared because it did not adapt to the changed customer lifestyle when motorcycles ceased to be a low cost alternative to cars and became a leisure, fun product for young people – supplied by Japanese competitors.

Glass container and can manufacturers saw themselves as being in those industries, and almost too late accepted that they were in the fast changing, innovative packaging business, competing with each other and also with plastic, paper and automatic dispensing alternatives.

The Swiss watch industry allowed new producers, using a different technology, to decimate their business. They did not research the basic needs of their customers nor their changing lifestyles, which increasingly made watches simply a fashion accessory and not the expensive masterpiece of yesteryear.

Summary

- Marketing is a *total* management philosophy. It is far more than selling or promotion; its impact must work right across a company or organisation to ensure a complete understanding of what the *customer* needs.

- The customer comes first.
- Profitability must be a strategic marketing goal – not simply making money, but ensuring that companies *survive* in a rapidly changing environment.

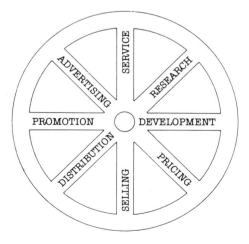

Figure 1

2
The marketing tools

Modern marketers are required to work with and utilise many elements. There is nothing to prevent any business – be it small or large, and whether engaged in marketing goods or services – from using the same elements to ensure that they are heading in the right direction.

Each of the elements, or components, of the marketing mix is important. Each can be adjusted to suit your particular type of business. The essential thing is to consider the application of the various elements – use them as a checklist each time you are about to plan an activity.

Look at Figure 1 on page 9. Imagine your business to be the hub of a wheel. The marketing elements are the spokes of that wheel.

In succeeding chapters, we will explore each element. But before we do, let us take a further look at those key items that we considered in the opening chapter.

Avoiding guesswork with research

Research is necessary to establish and check directions; to determine what is required; to measure performance.

Research allows us to identify our strengths and weaknesses, to uncover opportunities, to isolate gaps (which may not be readily apparent until we start digging) for profitable entry with goods or services.

The acceptability of marketing strategies related to other elements (for example, 'Are our selling methods efficient?' 'Is our advertising reaching the desired audience?') can be checked using research.

By ensuring that research is applied on an ongoing basis, a company can avoid the risk of becoming process or product oriented. Instead, wisely, it is listening to its market.

Research needs to be the starting point. It monitors the other elements, permits flexibility, and ensures that you are alert to the changes dictated by a fickle market place. The process need not be complex, overly sophisticated or grossly expensive. As we delve into the topic more thoroughly, we will discover just how much useful research can be carried out using your own resources.

Keeping ahead of the game with development

Nothing stands still. The aim is to become involved with products, services and markets that fit in with the things we do well or are capable of carrying out profitably.

Development does not necessarily mean brand-new products or services. An excellent market may exist for an improved or amended product or service; profitability may be enhanced by abandoning some activities.

Development considerations may spearhead diversification – not only into new product or service spheres but also into new markets, be they groups of customers we would like to reach or geographical regions at home or abroad.

Ensuring we are in the right place at the right time

Pricing requires distinct strategies that may vary for different markets, buyers and product areas. Maybe we could sum it up as: 'The right product in the right place at the right time – and at the right price.'

Distribution – getting ourselves into the market place

How do we 'move' our products or services from origination point to end-user? In Chapter 6 we will prove that distribution means far more than transport.

Making the sale – selling

'Nothing happens till somebody sells something.' Selling is important to the execution of the marketing mix. Selling is far more, today, than getting orders or closing deals.

We need to structure effective, economical sales methods that relate to distribution goals.

Telling our story – advertising, promotion and public relations

How do we convey our messages? How do we motivate people to purchase or use our wares or facilities? Essentially, we are talking about communication – the need to tell the market what we are up to.

Impact and memorability must be achieved. Internal audiences (your own people) may require just as much education as external readers, listeners or viewers.

As society increasingly directs piercing questions and criticism at the business sector, a well-planned corporate-affairs programme is a must for many companies.

Providing the extra edge – service and after-sales service

This is essential if we want to achieve sound, ongoing trading. So many purchase decisions are not influenced by price alone. 'Service' becomes the criterion, and service can be judged by a host of factors including quality, reliability, delivery terms, margins for retailers, and stock holding of spare parts.

Each of the elements outlined can be broken down into elaborate detail and applied as required. However, the simple approach to bear in mind is the seven 'ingredients' of the mix.

3

Research – doing your 'homework'

Let us say a manufacturer discovers that he can make an excellent mousetrap. So he produces thousands of mousetraps, then expects people to buy. What our would-be rodent mogul should first have determined is whether or not the public has a reasonable level of need for the dispatch of mice – the demand factor. He should also have checked their preferred dispatch method (cat versus trap). And do people want a product that is cheaper, better or longer-lasting?

This is why our marketing mix starts with research. Think of it as 'homework', and devote a healthy proportion of your time to making doubly sure that the way you are structuring your business and promoting your goods or services is in line with what the market place needs and what is profitable to your operation.

Marketing – and marketing research in particular – should be a very inquisitive craft. We must constantly remember not to take market factors for granted. Thus marketing is primarily concerned with questions: asking questions of the company; directing them at customers and intermediaries; reviewing products and services. This is the foundation required in order to ascertain strengths and weaknesses and uncover opportunities.

Do not be fooled by fancy terms such as 'gap analysis'. Just say to yourself: 'We're constantly on the look-out for new opportunities'. Such opportunities are achieved via a constant 'ear-to-the-ground' approach.

Research saves money

View research as an investment rather than an expense. It is far cheaper to spend a few thousand pounds finding out that a market does not exist or that a product is not quite right than to commit enormous expenditure to a full-scale launch – only to find out that you are heading down the wrong track or that you are too late or too expensive.

The very word 'research' tends to frighten many people. Yet research need not be complex or expensive. Nevertheless, the aura of mystique persists.

One useful definition that sums up the research role is: 'A systematic, objective and exhaustive search for and study of the facts relevant to *any* problem in the marketing field.'

Research means an ongoing search, a continual analysis. It can be internal (studying trends emerging from, for example, sales reports and other regularly compiled performance documents) or external (gathering data from the market place).

Quantitative research, which concentrates on numbers, should not necessarily take precedence over qualitative research – probing peoples' opinions, attitudes, etc.

You can do much research yourself

In urging business people to use simple, ongoing research methods, it is necessary to point out that an organisation's own personnel can often carry out a great deal of research, provided you accept that you are using the 'tool' to improve your knowledge. Do not expect research to provide absolute information every time. You are still expected to make the final decision or judgement!

Apart from using your own resources (manual or computerised) to calculate product, area or customer contributions, this 'proving' principle can extend to measuring awareness or checking a few basic facts via questionnaires or telephone contact.

In the industrial business-to-business field especially, there is an advantage in knowing that a small base is frequently representative. Moreover, the company that goes to the trouble of investigating its performance by seeking customers' opinions is very often perceived as caring. Taking pains to find out what people think about you can improve your mana with customers and potential customers. And the higher you climb the management tree, in terms of respondents' status, the better the feedback. Senior management personnel are generally sensible, articulate people.

The aim of industrial research is not to find out which lavatory cleaner is preferred by nine out of ten suburban households. To illustrate an application: a company supplying expensive capital equipment to, say, primary-product processors, wishes to determine whether or not the market is viable. It is likely that a selective base of freezing works or dairy factories may well provide adequate benchmarks. While the market value and volume is being ascertained, it is a relatively easy task to include further probes in the interviews. These may be designed to obtain feedback on competition and how customers perceive your service, delivery or pricing structures. What are customers'/potential customers' criteria for awarding contracts? Who makes decisions? And who *influences* decisions?

Extensions, as required, can be launched into learning more about the type of media that best communicate to your markets. Are special training programmes needed to ensure adequate machine familiarity? If so, how should these be administered?

Research need not be a high-price/occasional-use commodity. If you sit down and think about what you need to learn, the answers can frequently be obtained in a relatively simple and efficient manner.

Having advised readers not to overlook 'own-effort' research, it must be acknowledged that there are still many instances when the research task requires the use of outside specialists. The matter of briefing such people and obtaining value for money then becomes paramount – but that is another story that we cover later when looking at how to get the best from outside advisers (Chapter 27).

At the other end of the scale from the professionals: do not overlook the wealth of free and low-cost data that abounds in libraries, associations, trade bodies, banks and government departments. In fact, for many, the quest for improved information probably could start in-house. The amount of valuable background information hidden in cabinets, report files and monthly trading documents can be surprising.

Do not get carried away with quantity. Spend more time ensuring that the *quality* of your 'homework' is as good as possible.

Examples

One of the authors ongoing involvement over ten years with a company internationally recognised as a leader in the field of specialised flexible packaging has permitted the introduction of much *cost-effective research, frequently using client's own personnel*. Projects have included:
- Attitude studies aimed at respondents from primary-product, industrial and general foodstuffs sectors.
- Awareness studies, using telephone contact, to obtain client-versus-competitor ratings and rankings, plus basic information on current trends and requirements.

In 1980 one of the world's largest travel companies wished to evaluate its development of a new Far East market.

A useful starting point was for research field-workers to approach various travel agencies as 'customers'. We were then able to rate the agencies in terms of customer interest, product preferences (i.e., which travel package/airline was promoted), pricing structures, and follow-up.

The results revealed numerous weaknesses. Consequently, we then developed a travel 'workshop' for agency managers. These workshops, sponsored by the client, were based on combatting the weaknesses uncovered by our research and were presented in main centres to travel agency managers.

The workshops proved highly successful; the criticisms, because they were based on facts and not hypotheses, were well accepted and appreciated – so much so that the managers asked if a further series of workshops could be developed to alert their agency staff to the type of complacency that was creeping into the industry.

A group of European manufacturers wished to determine *promotional strategies* for countries such as New Zealand and Australia. During the measurement of customers' awareness of relevant literature, a total of 106 different publications were nominated/recalled.

As a result, we learned that overseas – i.e., European or American – journals commanded the most respect; that our principals should simply maintain their international-edition advertising; and that occasional newsletters should be despatched to update Australian and New Zealand customers.

Without the research, the principals may well have wasted money by embarking on special regional advertising campaigns. The overall cost for the newsletters for Australia and New Zealand was a fraction of that which would have been incurred producing and placing magazine advertisements.

Warranty cards returned to manufacturers supply a base of potential customers – especially if you manufacture a wide range of products or promote a variety of services. The same cards can be designed to encourage comments from buyers.

Likewise, a *thank you letter* to a new customer enclosing a reply-paid envelope and a brief questionnaire can uncover a number of rating factors to check your company's image, efficiency, trading policies or whatever.

Summary

The examples given embody pertinent lessons:

- The studies were not unduly expensive.

- The data was valuable in that it helped devise accurate marketing strategies – thus avoiding wasted pounds or funds directed into the wrong media.

- The clients were able to ensure that their 'products' were 'right' before their release.

- Intermediaries – in the case of the travel supplier – were educated in a manner based on facts. This, in turn, ensured that the link between the supplier and the end-user was efficient and effective.

Whether using mail, telephone or face-to-face techniques, ensure that research is designed to provide useful information and that the information is *used*. It must not be left to gather dust or, if problems emerge, not acted upon in the hope that the problems will run away. They will not.

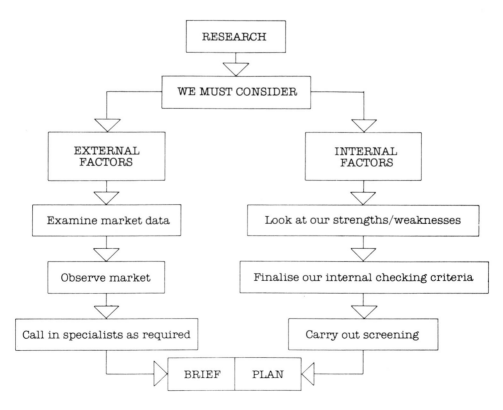

Figure 2

4

New directions – profitable development

Reducing risk should be one cardinal tenet of marketing. Research will help to pin-point what is required by the markets; development must be designed to capitalise on the opportunities uncovered or to combat any negatives that emerge.

When thinking about developments, do not be besotted with entirely *new* directions. Adjustments or slight modifications to existing products or services are also developmental strategies. In fact, the existing markets held should never be neglected at the expense of becoming overly interested in securing new business.

Quite apart from putting products or services under the microscope, development procedures should measure the regions or territories (locally and overseas) that comprise markets.

Diversification is a further useful prompt for keeping progressive management alert. Lateral thinking and creative flair is the order of the day. Brand new – and possibly outrageous – opportunities should be at the very least discussed. Companies need to avoid a staid, repetitive approach to predicting their future; tunnel vision must not be permitted.

'Think-tank' or 'task-force' approaches can be instituted easily and economically. There is no commitment, apart from time. Rather, regular diversification reviews should be held, designed to ensure that, periodically, new opportunities to make money or bring about increased efficiencies are thoroughly assessed. Such a creative, far-sighted view can only help companies to move forward.

Think creatively – avoid tunnel vision

A review group can be set up in an organisation to meet at regular intervals. In between review sessions, evaluations can be carried out.

Occasional, informal brainstorming sessions will soon teach people to think laterally.

As a simple guide, bear in mind problem-solving ('What do we need to improve?') and horizontal and vertical integration. *Horizontal integration* simply means spreading our risk at the same level but with different products or services – e.g., suppliers of plastic film packaging may decide to incorporate cardboard cartons in their range. After all, their business surrounds packaging/protection/presentation.

Likewise, chocolate could complement boiled sweets; bedroom furniture may dovetail with lounge furniture. The glory of the horizontal approach is that it opens new avenues for trade, frequently with the same customers. You don't need to be a genius to realise that, if you are detailing a supermarket with three products instead of one, you increase your chances of closing a sale.

Vertical integration allows us to explore the benefit of developing backwards and forwards in the cycle from production through to consumption. For example, a manufacturer who delivers goods to stores might investigate the viability of forming a transport subsidiary. A furniture factory might move forward in the chain by establishing its own retail furnishing store or backwards by acquiring a timber mill.

Development to ensure we do not stagnate

The overriding philosophy to guide your developmental group should be 'What might fit in with some of our company's products to help protect our future?'

When meeting to carry out the reviews, the format could be to divide the session into two parts. Section one would comprise the listing of ideas. Wild suggestions should be encouraged; there should be no criticism of the ideas presented; there should be no in-depth discussion.

Try to ensure that the group is on the look-out for unsatisfied or unconscious needs, and that 'me-too' situations are avoided.

It is in the second stage that the ranking or evaluation of the 'ideas' takes place – and *do not* take on too many tasks at once. Select a handful of priorities; delegate further evaluations, initially using your own resources.

The cost of all this is minimal, but its impact on morale can be tremendous. And if you strike the jackpot or, in the medium term, open a Pandora's box of new opportunity, what more could you ask?

With all approaches to development, sensible commercial risk must prevail. Realistic appraisal, research with defined cut-off points, a pilot or trial approach to test the market – these are some of the control stages that ensure matters do not get out of hand.

Development-oriented reviews force us to seek ways to improve company performance and productivity.

Objectivity may well lead to a better marketing organisation, improved product/service design, and development initiative – heeding the life cycles of your range and being ready to offer replacements (or drop unprofitable lines).

Relationships with suppliers, customers and your own personnel can be improved – and a sounder approach can be established to the company's finance and investment procedures.

Investigating new directions and avoiding complacency will become second nature if a sensible development philosophy is allowed to flourish.

Summary

Developing new or improved *products or services*; developing new *markets*; identifying and developing profitable *segments or niches* within the market – these are essential management functions.

Time invested in development planning reduces the risk of failure – and some statistics have rated new product failure rates as high as 95 per cent.

Key steps are as follows:

- Broad evaluation.

- Study market – customers, competitors, regulations.

- Double-check desire/acceptability for product or service.

- Check that your organisation's structure is geared to handle new developments.

- Check raw materials supply, production capacity.

- Check costings and pricing.

- Check distribution, packaging, labelling.

- Evaluate and determine promotion and advertising requirements.

- Determine follow-up service.

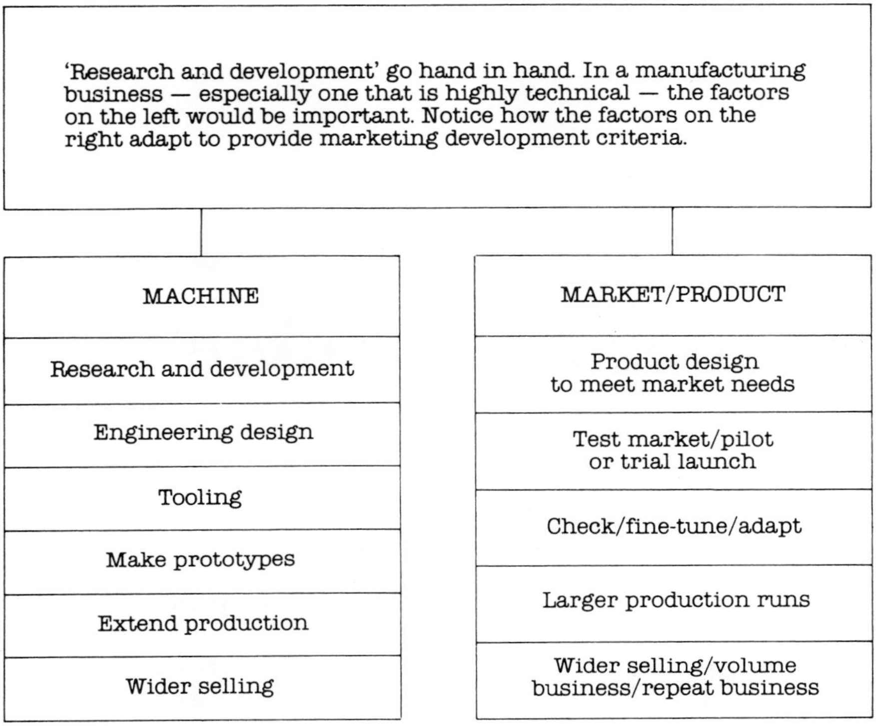

'Research and development' go hand in hand. In a manufacturing business — especially one that is highly technical — the factors on the left would be important. Notice how the factors on the right adapt to provide marketing development criteria.

MACHINE	MARKET/PRODUCT
Research and development	Product design to meet market needs
Engineering design	Test market/pilot or trial launch
Tooling	Check/fine-tune/adapt
Make prototypes	Larger production runs
Extend production	Wider selling/volume business/repeat business
Wider selling	

Figure 3

5
Pricing – think of a number and double it?

Driving to a business meeting recently, the car petrol gauge looked alarmingly low. This stimulated the thought of how the pricing of a commodity product like oil could be so complex. The actual cost of production becomes almost insignificant against demand levels, output quotas, government legislation on duties and taxes, political considerations in the Middle East.

Over the past two decades, oil prices have moved from virtually an exploitation level in the 1960s, to a high that shook the world's financial stability to its foundations in the seventies, and then almost back to rock bottom in the 1980s, as usage fell and suppliers attempted to hold their production levels via the price cutting route.

If prices are pushed too high, even on an essential like oil, customers will find ways of fighting back.

To put it another way: most of us are generally balanced on a commercial tightrope. Most of us do not want to plunge from that perch. We need a safety net. One safety net is to ensure that the pricing of our goods or services is not a hit-and-miss affair.

Price is important – but not necessarily most important

As we have noted earlier, price is not the sole criterion on which customers base purchase decisions. However, it is important to the supplier in that the amount charged directly affects how much the company will earn. Earning performance is, admittedly, also governed by aspects other than price – reducing overheads can contribute to bottom-line improvements, as can increased productivity.

Many manufacturers fret over waste in the form of production rejects or surplus. Yet the same industrialists often spend insufficient time worrying about the direction in which they are steering their company. Waste extends beyond the factory floor to human resources, money and time – and lost opportunities.

Pricing – many techniques

We have all heard the oft-quoted expression, 'He charges like a wounded bull.' That is not what is advocated here. Pricing is complex, and the determination of levels frequently requires the pooled resources of marketing, production and financial management. Specific pricing strategies should be the order of the day, governed by numerous considerations that may include the market-place situation and trading climate, competitors' pricing, and assorted bases for price-setting.

Those price-setting bases might, in turn, be influenced by any one of several factors: Do we apply a cost-plus approach? Is this a case for marginal costing? On the other hand, if we have developed a market-oriented product or service, perhaps a unique or very specialist application, we may have a case for opportunity pricing – a 'What will the market bear?' technique.

And as far as volume business from regular sources is concerned: do we reduce our prices? Or can we figure a quantitative discount scheme to encourage larger offtakes?

As stated before, pricing is a complex element. Any marketer worth his or her salt must be aware of the influence of price on the marketing mix. It gets right back to our original contention that marketing must have a profit focus.

Life cycles for products or services could be one facet for the marketer's attention in establishing pricing strategies. Life cycles cover introductory, growth, maturity, saturation and decline phases.

It is fashionable to chatter away about cash cows, dogs, lemons and so on. But, when everything's brought back to basics, it is simply the jargon that has changed – we are really talking about winners versus losers, profitable versus unprofitable.

Depending on demand, uniqueness and the like, you may be called upon to make high investments and accept low profits or, at the other end of the scale, reap sound profits once your product/service is well accepted.

Demand factor

The major governing factor is whether the markets are growing or declining because of demand changes. Remember, we talked about people's needs. Imagine an enormous demand for boiled, sugar-coated hedgehogs. Is this demand going to last for one, five or ten years? The starting point is obvious: sit down and plot a sales-and-profit curve using value and time guidelines. Then link your product-market strategies.

Pricing on some lines (except those deliberately used as a 'bait' to gain further sales revenue from other purchases) may be suicidal – with the result that product/service deletions would be a sensible step.

Price reductions might even create more volume – will they mean longer production runs, economies of scale and, in turn, more profit?

As with so many marketing angles, questions emerge – which brings us back to gaining knowledge through researching – doing our homework.

Sensible, survivor companies must be able to analyse and quantify. They need to be right up with the play in terms of cash flow, gross earnings and expenses, profit and loss. Combined with market intelligence, this helps identify whether deletions, modifications or replacements are required – and at what price.

Summary

- Pricing and costing are important because what we charge has a direct bearing on how much money we shall make.

- Price is important, but it is *not necessarily the most important factor* governing a purchasing decision. Pricing, quality, reliability, service, etc. must all blend together.

6

Improving sales and distribution

Libraries bulge with volumes on how to sell. There are people getting rich on public-speaking circuits by revealing the latest, best, most miraculous ways of ensuring that the customer or prospect says 'Yes'. Do not expect to find amazing revelations within this chapter – it is not marketing's style. You should, however, have a few useful and pertinent points reinforced.

Having, at the outset of this book, stated a desire to avoid the academic and distil the practical, this may be an opportune place to record a few background points and rules that fit in with the scheme of marketing.

By now, readers who were previously a little fuzzy as to what marketing is really about should have a clearer picture. Marketing is no phenomenon of recent years; it has been with us since earliest trading days, albeit in a different guise – less pigeon-holed in definitional terms.

Although, as we have already observed, marketing is not selling, the act of securing an order or closing a sale has to be acknowledged as an essential ingredient. The combination of all the marketing-mix elements to achieve best effects at minimum cost would be wasted if, at the end of the day, no sales were realised.

Isolate your best areas of return

If asked to provide succinct guidelines to aid the process of sales and distribution, experience over the years would suggest two guiding statements. The first is *Pareto's law* (sometimes referred to as the 80/20 rule or theory). Essentially, it reminds us that 80 per cent of sales may come from 20 per cent of customers (or 80 per cent of problems from 20 per cent of customers?). The numbers are not meant to be absolute. What the Pareto effect means is that a small proportion can have a disproportionate influence on the whole.

The second principle, based on the *Ansoff matrix*, simplifies the setting of sales objectives by concentrating on just two dimensions – what is sold and who will buy. The framework reminds us that we can sell:

- Existing products to existing customers.
- New products to existing customers.
- Existing products to new customers.
- New products to new customers.

Together, the two principles emphasise that, before one goes thundering into the market place seeking new business, existing opportunities deserve full exploitation.

It costs money to achieve sales . . . so ensure effectiveness

The high cost of retaining salespeople, and their propensity to change employers, means that sales forces should be of minimum size and maximum professionalism. They should be organised and deployed with as much precision as possible, trained and directed, accustomed to concentrating on customers and prospects holding the most potential.

The days of the order-taker or patterned, 'Hi, what do you want this trip?' salesman are history. With today's discerning buyers, salespeople need to possess consummate skills. Frequently, they must be technical advisers; always, they should be problem-solvers. Their wares will benefit someone – that is, fulfil somebody's need or provide a solution to a problem.

Salespeople should develop on appreciation and understanding of marketing skills (which, after all, embody selling yet extend much further) and be caught up in the marketing philosophy. They are the eyes and ears of the company in the market place – the company's 'bristling antennae', as one excellent and accurate description, which I first heard from a university dean, puts it.

Because salespeople are at the commercial mine-face, their ability to report accurately, precisely and promptly about what is happening in the field is paramount. So is their individual attention to planning – preparation, priorities, call cycles, ranking customers to determine contact frequency, and contact methods.

Selling does not necessarily mean physical contact. The utilisation of low-cost, effective, sales-reminder aids is a must. To what extent, then, is the telephone used to aid sales efforts? And we do not mean having a secretary or canvasser phone up to arrange a cold appointment. This doubtful technique, increasingly used by life insurance salespeople and purveyors of frequently dubious home-improvement aids, is not the stuff of marketing.

Sales liaison deserves scrutiny as a support item or reorder reminder. Telephone use, mail drops and assorted sales aids are excellent ammunition to complement the selling arsenal.

Salespeople's requirements vary across the board. An industrial or technical salesperson would display differing characteristics from those people expected to sell retail goods in a store or everyday consumer goods to assorted outlets.

The industrial type of sales approach demands initiative and planning – identifying and developing prime prospects. Often, the industrial salesperson's role can best be filled by a technician-turned-salesperson. As products, services or systems accelerate in complexity, so too does the advisory task increase. Some products could, for example, demand a graduate in sciences or computer studies.

Once we reach the plateau that calls for a higher reward level related to higher qualifications, we must ensure total effectiveness. As long as productivity in salespeople remains difficult to measure, the importance of Pareto's law and the Ansoff matrix cannot be over-emphasised.

Avoid wasting time, effort and money

Our American friends have developed succinct phrases to describe sales philosophy. Two that should be embedded in our subconscious are 'using a rifle instead of a shotgun' and 'defensive selling'. These are simple yet very worthwhile reminders: the former advocating that we select our market niches or segments, the latter compelling us to protect our existing, known markets and to exploit our existing customers before racing after new business.

Marketing can help us to avoid random, wasteful forays. It does not promote hard selling. What it does encourage is an aggressive, positive, *planned* approach. Salespeople today must be intelligent, thinking people, not fast talkers. They should be able to cross-sell and up-sell; they need to be familiar with added value. They must appreciate that they are the pivot points for a marketing information and intelligence system; they must be able to identify with their customers. Otherwise, they have no right to call themselves salespeople.

Selling must be linked with other elements

The expectations surrounding distribution techniques must be constantly evaluated. If marketing in one sense equals the movement of a concept through to an end-user, then the way in which product or service is distributed – or channelled – emerges as a key link.

Some aspects of distribution dovetail with selling and, for that matter, promotion. An advertisement or direct-mail piece may, for example, invite a reply or elicit an order and thus take over the 'sales' role.

Physical distribution costs continue to escalate. Astute business people must evaluate transport and storage methods, dispatch techniques, and the advantages and disadvantages of completely or partly knocked-down goods versus assembled products. All too often, the distribution perusal stops at inventory and shipping – storage and movement.

These physical aspects aside, distribution has a further dimension: channels – not only the direct channels that the supplier may be able to control but also the indirect channels. It is here that the role of the intermediary surfaces.

Never overlook intermediaries

Intermediaries, whether they be distributors, agents or any other form of middlemen, are a growing force to ensure reach to markets. Apart from the actual selling function carried out by, for example, an agent, there are 'non-selling' intermediaries who are able to influence sales. An architect would be a classic example of a person who is able to 'refer' business back to a supplier simply by recommending a type of building material to the client.

The intermediaries are as important as the end-users in 'market' terms. In fact, the intermediary is frequently your consumer and must be won over, motivated and enthused if you are to succeed.

Establishments that accept credit cards for settlement on behalf of the cards' issuers further illustrate the need to motivate the 'link' as we witness more and more people carrying a variety of credit cards (all of which probably fulfil the charging task equally well).

The acid-test question for a company pondering distribution alternatives is whether or not one's own resources should be used. Do we sell directly or use intermediaries? Specialist intermediaries are sometimes better geared than the producer to realise penetration into market sectors; in other instances, because they carry so many lines, these same intermediaries can be accused of paying little attention to specific suppliers whom they are contracted to represent.

Where organisations do rely on intermediaries such as agents or distributors, strict control is essential. Both the principal and the intermediary are accountable to each other. Properly drawn-up agreements, joint planning, and regular reporting systems are just three things that need to be established – yet they are generally dismissed as being unnecessary (the 'avoid paperwork at all costs' syndrome).

Unpleasant issues arise when principal and intermediary have what they describe as a 'gentleman's agreement'. Deals carried in the head or cemented with a handshake are not effective. Each party's obligations must be clearly set out.

In the next chapter we continue to stress the importance of making the most of 'marketing partnerships'.

7

Sharing risk and expanding horizons

High money costs, combined with the need to finance growth rather than be overtaken by competitors, forces us to look at alternative expansionary tactics. In recent years, there has been growing awareness of shared responsibilities via franchising, joint equity, and licensing-type arrangements.

The case for franchising, especially, is relatively simple. Franchising allows the franchisor fast coverage on a widespread or national scale for products and services. Most of the necessary capital is subscribed by the franchisee who, as a self-employed person, is usually motivated to work hard at developing a successful business.

At the same time, the franchisee is frequently entering into business with a tried-and-tested product or service. Sometimes a relatively modest amount of capital is required; often, previous experience is not necessary.

High standards all round

Education, training and high-quality standards are frequently the corner-stones of franchises. Franchisors realise the importance of motivation and excellence – the McDonald's and Kentucky Fried Chickens of this world did not get where they are today through second-rate achievements.

Satisfied, energetic, money-making franchisees provide a better return for the franchisor if ongoing royalty payments are part of the deal. Consequently, it is important that everybody understands from the outset what is expected and what is provided.

Supervision can, if handled incorrectly, create problems. After all, the franchisor's saying, 'Here's your chance to run your own business' – and then requesting that all sorts of reporting procedures and guidelines be observed. Some feeling can emerge on the franchisee's part that the anticipated independence is not quite up to scratch.

The need for controls to protect all parties must be spelled out. It is in franchisees' best interests that their standards be checked – reply-paid customer questionnaires, on-location observations by franchisor executives and 'mystery customer' visits followed by an assessment are just a few ways of obtaining feedback. The involvement by the franchisor demonstrates interest and enables day-to-day operating problems to be covered. At the same time, forthcoming developments, individual standards – and how they relate to wider parameters – can be elaborated.

To keep all matters on track, proper agreements are without doubt a key factor. The loose approach simply does not pay off. Legal experts or advisers who specialise in developing franchising or joint-venture plans should be used for guidance.

Detailed agreements and conditions

All franchise, agency and distribution set-ups – in fact any form of joint-responsibility structure – should have a well-thought-out approach to policy matters, promotional aids, training, back-up and support, exclusivity and territorial definitions.

As the programme develops, a series of documented plans should be available for review – concerning objectives; the basis for initial and ongoing franchisee fees or commissions; levies and payments; recruitment, training and advertising policies; cash projections; and controls. These are some of the important matters that one would expect to find outlined so that each party is aware of its responsibilities and obligations.

In essence, a shared undertaking is another form of trading link – another 'marketing partnership' that depends on mutual support.

Irrespective of the manner in which expansion or wider coverage might be achieved, the guiding principle throughout is to explore improvements that may result from a new approach to, or elimination of, middlemen. Too many middlemen equals less profit. But is this always the case? A specialist agent may open doors that the principal cannot.

You will hear it said that distributors frequently handle so many lines that they cannot pay proper attention to any of them; that commission salespeople neglect service aspects. This is too often true. And yet the 'middleman' schemes can work for small companies *provided* agreements are enforced and respected by each participating side.

Careful evaluation of all options should be undertaken by companies seeking to expand their trading reach. Those options can embrace increasing their own efforts, appointing agents or distributors, and developing franchises or some other form of licensing agreement.

Decide where you want the company or organisation to be in, say, five years. Then review the alternatives available in terms of near and more distant future and their bearing on your current situation.

Checklist: how to develop a franchising agreement

1 **The overall plan:**
Aims, objectives.

2 **Legal aspects:**
Agreement, rights.

3 **Financial aspects:**
Initial and ongoing fees, levies, payment methods.
Financial projections – cash flows, profit levels, capital requirements.
Finance plans – e.g., assistance with leasing equipment etc.

4 **Organisation and administration aspects:**
Recruitment and training of personnel.
Job descriptions.
Evaluation methods.
Back-up and personnel support.

5 **Location aspects:**
Territorial, area rights.
Expansion rights.

6 **Promotional programmes:**
Assorted advertising – corporate support, regional 'drives', etc.
Promotional aids and merchandising.
Public relations activities.
'Internal' communication links between franchisor and franchisee.

Checklist: how to develop an agent distributor agreement

1 **Commissions and fees:**
Including procedures in event of indirect sales – e.g., direct orders to manufacturer.
Payment levels and methods, payment periods.

2 **Prices and terms:**
Including any quantitative, bulk-buying or 'early payment' discounts.

3 **Right to purchase and sell products:**
Manufacturer's (i.e., principal's) products that may be sold.

4 **Industries and customer types:**
Those sectors that agent/distributor is expected to concentrate upon in terms of

selling, development, promotion, etc.

5 **Territories:**
Region/s within which agent/distributor is permitted to operate.

6 **Principal's undertakings:**
Deliveries, shipments, adequate packaging, transportation, etc.
Warranties.
Claims situations, procedures regarding defects etc., who bears costs, credits, replacement goods.
Product changes, modifications, price adjustments, etc. – procedure regarding notice and advice to agent/distributor.

7 **Advertising, promotional support, sales aids:**
Price lists, sales manuals, technical bulletins or data sheets (where appropriate), samples, etc.
Media advertising support– proportion contribution by agent/distributor where/if applicable.
Field assistance from principal – e.g., customer visits with agent/distributor.

8 **Technical assistance (where applicable):**
Laboratory tests, trials, development projects, field/plant checks, etc. for agent/distributor, on customers' behalf.

9 **Education and training:**
Support from principal, general training, familiarity visits to plant, ongoing training.

10 **Agent/distributor undertakings:**
To carry out tasks to achieve agreed aims.
Display and service facilities (where applicable).
Calibre, quantity of sales personnel to achieve aims.
Order quantities.
Product range to be carried.
Payment terms, time frames, and methods.
Protection for principal against claims by third parties, avoidance by agent/distributor of any actions or trading practices that could harm principal's name or goodwill or be detrimental to customers' or public interest.
Agent/distributor not to copy any of principal's products or pass information to other manufacturers or competitors.
Agent/distributor not to carry products directly competitive to those supplied by principal.

11 **Trademarks, registered names or brands:**
Limits and rules regarding use.

12 **Reporting, sales budgets and market information:**
Monthly and other periodic reporting requirements re-

garding sales, competitors' activities, promotional activities, special projects, general market intelligence, etc.

13 **Termination of agreement:**
Method of serving notice.
Time frame from serving notice until termination effective.
Termination *without* notice – applications and situations where this applies.
Settlement of outstanding monies at termination of agreement.
Procedure regarding return of products, support items, promotional aids, etc. to principal in event of termination.

14 **Conditions following termination of agreement:**
Situation regarding agent/distributor's losing right to refer to principal's product names or to any standing as an authorised agent/distributor for principal.
Agent/distributor not to handle any products similar to those marketed by principal for a period of time, as defined in agreement.

8
Motivating the sales force

A business magazine editor once asked us for an article on sales force motivation. We agreed but emphasised that sales planning was something that required a much more detailed approach. Planning comes first because in our opinion, you can motivate until the cows come home, but if you are not motivating in relationship to planned goals the effort may be wasted.

Considerable expense is involved in maintaining a full-time representative. Frequent cost-of-living adjustments, increments based on promotion and achievement, plus high vehicle running and replacement costs leave their mark. Hiking your price is not always practical. So, what is the answer?

A planned approach to selling

No single word sums up the solution. However, if we acknowledge that high costs per call are here to stay, then the secret must lie in concentrating on improved score rates and reduced overheads (but not at the expense of servicing). Part of the answer then must emerge from a pre-planned, carefully-thought-out approach to selling.

Remember, the aim of just about every sale goes beyond closing on a single occasion. Repeat business is the name of the game. The transaction, what is more, involves two parties – the buyer and the seller. Let us call our buyer 'the customer' and make it quite clear that, in today's competitive and questioning market place, the customer is right at the top of the totem pole.

This being the case, salespeople who pride themselves on their professional approach must define, uncover and get to grips with their customers' problems. The next step is to promote your products or services as solutions to those problems.

Numerous evaluations conducted in the market place tend to leave the impression that what we preach is not practised. Too frequently, one gets the feeling that salespeople believe that they are doing the buyer/ customer a favour. There is almost a 'take it or leave it' approach best illustrated by that disgusting shop-assistant phrase 'Can I help you?' To which the obvious response has to be 'No'.

Take the store parallel a step further. What happens when a customer strikes somebody who appears to be genuinely interested in satisfying his or her need? The customer goes back; the customer tells his or her friends. So two benefits emerge: repeat business and word-of-mouth advertising (the latter absolutely free and more believable than the slickest television commercial).

It is a buyers' not a sellers' market

We have, in most cases, a trading climate that can be labelled a buyers' market. A primary requisite of the sales force's role is to make sure that whatever it is you are selling stands out from the crowd of ever-increasing, frequently look-alike offers.

To this end, you must sell beyond the order book or catalogue. You must sell quality, service, and a genuinely caring attitude.

Learn to categorise your customers. Before charging into the market place to ferret our new business, make absolutely sure that you are exploiting existing business thoroughly.

Review your customer mix frequently. If you are selling a high percentage of volume to one category, ensure that category is being covered thoroughly before moving on to others. As we have already mentioned, Pareto's law – or the 80/20 theory – reminds us that 80 per cent of our business comes from 20 per cent of our customers. And 80 per cent of good sales from 20 per cent of the sales force? Now there is food for sales managers' thought . . .

Way beyond order-taking

Planning one's approach to selling not only means ranking customers and plotting call cycles and frequencies. It also involves deeper analysis – of how time is spent (actual selling versus preparing reports, travelling, etc.); how profitable various lines are to the company (liaise closely with financial people); and what the most effective way of reaching customer groups is (face to face, letter or telephone).

Improved recording methods are essential. Call lists and call reports, properly maintained and sensibly structured, can disgorge a wealth of history, painting a rapid picture charting progress (or otherwise) with customers. Accurate, quantified input allows extrapolation of patterns and trends.

Far too many salespeople misguidedly believe that their job is to write business. Agreed, that is part of their job – important too – but it is not enough. These same types will quickly protest that sales planning and reporting is a waste of time and money. If you or your people really believe this, then you are fooling yourselves. The planners – those who calculate and examine their own efforts and the performance of their products (and competitors' products) – are the ones who succeed.

Interestingly enough, we usually find that the folk who decry a more professional approach to selling are the same people who, when sales targets are not being realised, point out defensively that the product is not right, the price is too high, or the competition is wheeling and dealing.

Such people need to realise that the trading climate is tougher, the market has changed, and competition – direct, indirect, local and international – is increasing.

Management obligations

Sales management must be aware of their increased responsibility to supervise, assist, train, and lead by sound example. And if that is not tied in with motivation, what is? To realise these things, a sales plan must exist – not in the mind, along with a raft of jokes to tell at the next sales conference, but as a tangible, *written* document that clearly sets out and rationalises objectives and strategies.

As well as budgets and targets, include time frames; explore and suggest new projects – systematic approaches to evaluate and realise new business opportunities.

Build in controls to enable you to measure progress towards meeting objectives, and to permit tactical adjustments to counter market shifts and drifts.

There must be at least a dozen methods of selling. As an exercise, write down the methods that you are employing. If the list is short, it could be high time that you started to professionalise your sales and sales-management approach. At the very least, be sufficiently open-minded to evaluate cost-effective, customer-oriented alternatives.

Motivation and incentive

To understand motivation, it is necessary to understand behaviour. Berelson and Steiner, in their *Human Behaviour: An Inventory of Scientific Findings*, say in part that 'human behaviour itself is so enormously varied, so delicately complex, so obscurely motivated that many people despair of finding valid generalisations to explain and predict the actions, thoughts and feelings of human beings'.

In essence: motivation is complex. Yet it is at the heart of sales management. It is the 'how to' of getting salespeople to perform more efficiently.

Granted, we need money. But we need far more. Abraham Maslow's 'Hierarchy of Needs' has taught many of us this. Money and incentives usually go hand in hand. Right? Wrong! Look at the tax structure for a start. If you have got a team that is motivated by money alone, start looking about quietly for replacements.

Incentives that motivate a genuine salesperson include challenge, interest, and a sense of belonging and participation. Opportunities to learn are important. After all, improvement frequently leads to salary and benefit upgrades. So, you see, the money need is taken care of after all, and not merely as a carrot-dangling exercise.

Sales direction, planning and motivation – to my mind, they are certainly interwoven, and they all boil down to supervision via leadership, example and an analytical, flexible approach that heeds the market and customers ahead of anything else.

Checklist: how to develop incentive programmes

When incentive programmes are introduced, they must not be hit-and-miss, half-hearted or amateurish affairs. Guidelines include:

1   Ensure that your products, pricing and market positions create realistic opportunity for goals or targets to be achieved by participants. Clarify taxation rulings.

2   Clearly define the extent of participation – is it solely sales force or beyond? What are the measurement criteria for non-sales effort?

3   Prepare a clear, concise, written plan and supporting schedule.

4   Assign responsibility for overall control to a senior person.

5   Plan timing carefully; allow sufficient time for goals to be realised.

6 Decide on realistic targets and scoring methods. Ensure equal chances for all – e.g., by territory-proportioning – to achieve a common denominator.

7 Set out programme rules clearly, leaving no room for misunderstanding.

8 Check that the types of awards envisaged are best suited to participants' aspirations.

9 If travel awards are included, ensure that all details, including destination arrangements, are completely arranged well in advance and that extra touches or special privileges are included.
(*Note:* Research carried out has indicated that travel is the strongest incentive. Travel prizes frequently appear to work hardest for the scheme sponsor.
The same could apply to consumer contests – in fact a number of the guidelines listed here could cover the preparation of a consumer contest.
In some studies, 98 per cent of the base rated travel incentives as successful and 36 per cent rated travel more highly than other motivational schemes; 94 per cent of the people who had built their incentive schemes around travel indicated that they would use travel again as an incentive.)

10 Select your prizes carefully (do not give away rubbish).

11 Prepare budgets to include your promotional and support costs, as well as prizes.

12 Establish proper record-keeping procedures.

13 Time the launch of the incentive programme to achieve greatest impact.

14 Plan a stimulating launch so that the programme starts on a high note.

15 Maintain interest throughout – circulate frequent progress reports or 'contest bulletins'.

Finally, although there can only be one overall winner, try to also include scatter prizes or a series of small awards.

And one last word of warning: before embracing incentive programmes, debate whether or not you might be grabbing a tiger by the tail. Think of breakfast-food marketing – kids throw out the cereal to pounce on the toys in the bag. . . .

Summary

- Motivation and productivity start with *sales planning*.

- The day of the order-taker is over. Salespeople must be top notch in regard to their:

  1 Product and company/business knowledge.

  2 Ability to home in on the best customers and avoid dissipation of effort.

  3 Understanding of marketing – their role as providers of benefits, problem-solvers.

  4 Understanding of their customers' business and requirements.

  5 Follow-up and service.

- Management must expect meaningful information from field people. We are all accountable – sales management to sales force and vice versa. The planning stressed earlier relies on accurate inputs to ensure accurate strategy formulation.

- Motivation does not simply mean offering more money. We must provide people with new *challenges*, increased *opportunities* and a feeling that they are *contributing* to the total effort.

9
Getting your message across

Whether we are talking about advertising, promotion, direct mail, merchandising, packaging or any of the plethora of 'devices' used to inform, motivate and advise a variety of publics about our business, goods, services, benefits or offers, we can be sure of one thing: we are *communicating*.

Communication is frequently the nub of marketing management – within and outside an organisation. Unfortunately, on the private front, most of us find it difficult to communicate properly. Small wonder, then, that when we are faced with the wider masses, all sorts of problems emerge.

Whereas research can, properly tuned, provide accurate results and conclusive evidence, it is difficult to maintain objectivity when it comes to the more 'visible' marketing tools. With advertising, for example, everybody feels they are an expert. Think of your friends who 'hate' or 'never watch' television advertising – the same friends will proceed to give a blow-by-blow description of a commercial for bathroom cleaner or detergent (accurately recalling the product name, the presenter's appearance, the voice-over accent, etc.).

We are of a generation that is able to beam mass communication to an audience of millions in a fraction of a second; we are blasé about highly technical production processes. The penalties continue: witness the communicative difficulties encountered in so many relationships – parents and children, husbands and wives, teachers and pupils. . . .

So, on the business front, is it any wonder that we find break-downs between employers and employees, and manufacturers and their customers or 'publics'?

Communication – active and silent

Communication – whether it be the active art or the label on a packet – is the manner in which we talk to those 'publics'.

If you have developed a product that is chock-full of exciting, new benefits, then you need to tell people (start by convincing your own staff or intermediaries) why it is bigger and better, or will save money, time, energy, etc. That communication is then carried via the media advertising, public relations, point-of-sale material, packaging, and so on.

These aspects must be designed to ensure that your products or services appeal to as many customers as possible – not forgetting the folk within your organisation or those upon whom you rely to reach your end-markets. If your staff and intermediaries are not convinced and motivated, if they do not believe the benefits and promises, how can you expect them to enthusiastically convince buyers that your offer is worthwhile?

Ensure you gain attention

The communication scenario is further complicated by wastage. Lord Leverhulme set people's minds working with his immortal statement that half his company's advertising was wasted – ah, but how to determine which half?

Consider the number of television channels, radio stations, news-papers, magazines, direct-mail pieces, and mobile and stationary advertisements you are subjected to – even subconsciously. Now include a few other factors: products multiply; the mind subtracts (how can we stand out from the crowds?); there are the effects of overkill – the bombardment of messages hammering at already-cluttered minds.

Add to this the fact that over 80 per cent of what we hear we forget within 24 hours. Do not overlook that most of us are very good talkers but comparatively poor listeners. The result is a rather complex process.

Be prepared to investigate imaginative ways of getting your message across. The most lavish and expensive is not necessarily best. Many managers simply engage in a show of pompous advertising to satisfy their ego. It is better to find out which media and which 'language' your market will respond to most favourably. What will they take notice of – not simply scan – and consider in depth? What will they deem believable?

Talking 'one to one'

Demonstration means a lot to audiences – hence the power of television. Demonstration does not necessarily mean expensive film production. Make use of audio-visuals, flip charts, participation in exhibitions and fairs – in other words, spend time thinking about ways to reach your audience on a personalised basis.

The more specialised your business, the less you need to rely on widespread or major media. There are media salespeople and in-competent media planners out there just waiting to waste *your* money. Avoid hit-and-miss efforts; spend more time on selectivity. When you do something, do it supremely well.

As an example of how to avoid waste: research studies that we have carried out have proved, in some powerful trading sectors, that industrial buyers place more emphasis on learning about product developments from overseas rather than 'home-grown' trade journals. They pay greater attention to local activities that emphasise the 'one to one' concept and basic demonstration.

Consequently, over the years, many clients have seen fit to develop, among other things, newsletters incorporating case studies (believability) and to utilise their operations or plant to demonstrate their business activities and capabilities.

Use your trading links

In the case of companies that enjoy links with parent organisations or affiliates abroad, a close working relationship with these partners is a must. Material produced overseas can be adapted for the 'home' market; visiting experts can be utilised for customer seminars; overseas develop-ments can be tested to measure local adaptability.

Essentially, every communication strategy needs to work hard for you. Many functions can perform dual roles – video aids are useful not only for exhibitions and sales presentations but also for training; co-operative promotions with intermediaries or retailers can give you extended mileage and permit your promotional spending to go further; postage can pay for account mailings that include sales reminders.

Total co-ordination

Image must work right across the board. That means you must not overlook items such as sign-writing on delivery vehicles, letterheads, business cards, packaging, and livery. Many of these aspects, where they apply to a business, help form impressions, favourable or otherwise, in the minds of your customers or potential customers. They are frequently 'silent salesmen'.

This brings us back, again, to stressing the importance of your own people. They can be walking, talking advertisements for your company –not just the sales force, but the entire team. The switchboard operator or receptionist is often the first image-influencer when somebody approaches a company; storemen talk to friends about where they work and what their companies are engaged in.

Develop in-house where possible

A great deal of communication material can be developed within your own organisation. Escalating production costs mean that it is basic common sense to handle projects using your own resources wherever possible. A company's own personnel – especially where there are technical or specialist overtones – may be better equipped to develop a message than a copywriter whose forte is flowery prose.

Nevertheless, for some projects, outside advisers and agencies should be used. However, such people must be viewed as being accountable to you, the client. It is your money, your reputation. The art of developing a sound working relationship and obtaining the best results from 'outsiders' is elaborated in a later section.

To round off these broad comments on communication, we again advocate the questioning approach. Starting from square one, ask yourself: What do we want to say? Where do we want to say it? To whom are we directing this message? When should we place our message? And so on.

Question the 'outsiders' responsible for preparing your campaigns: Why has our campaign been devised in this manner? Has it been tested? What's our rationale? Why are we spending this amount of money? Why have these media been selected? What benefits can we expect? Do we need to spend more – or could we, in fact, spend less? What are competitors up to?

Do not simply accept the 'we've always done it this way' or 'they must know; they're experts' cop-outs.

Last – but certainly not least – do not ever, ever discount the tremendous value of word-of-mouth communication. Strive to build a profile that occasions people to say 'Bloggs and Bloggs are good people to do business with'. Word-of-mouth advertising or recommendation is still the best, most credible, least expensive form of communication around.

An example of specialist communication

One of the world's leading travel and entertainment card companies wished to re-examine its total advertising. Media used included television, press, magazine and radio.

Recommendations were based on combatting the lack of one-to-one 'written' communication with?

1 Card members.
2 Those outlets that accepted the client's card.

The 'tools' devised were specialist newsletters and bulletins designed to keep card-users and intermediaries informed on card policies, new services and benefits, and card applications. For 'trade' publications, assorted business hints were also included.

Over the next seven years, the techniques were further refined. During that period, tracking-study research included monitoring the impact, awareness and memorability of the devices to aid forward planning.

This form of specialist communication has continued to be a major item in the company's overall marketing approach. Computer programs and mailing techniques have been refined to a 'state of the art' level ensuring that projects embody speed and *accuracy*.

Your company does not need to be a world leader in order to utilise such techniques. Travel, furniture, home appliances and financial services are just four categories where adaptation of the principles outlined has proved valuable and successful.

The main ingredients are a word processor, a simple storage/retrieval system, and common sense:

- People who take one trip usually start dreaming about their next adventure shortly after returning home.
- Business travellers can be candidates for personal or family excursions.
- People who buy lounge suites could, in due course, be interested in carpet, dining or bedroom furniture.
- Furniture and appliances have 'lives'; reminders regarding replacement or upgrading items, along with occasional releases 'cross-selling' your product range, show that you are interested in your customer.
- Today's borrower is tomorrow's investor.

Checklist: how to develop communication strategies

1 What *benefits* are offered by our products or services? Are there any *advantages* over other products/services? Is there anything *unique*?

2 *Who* and *where* are our prime target markets?

3 What will be our *key message*?

4 Profile product/service purchasers and users, and those who may *influence* the purchase or use of our product/service.

5 Set out *competitor activities*. How are competitors' products/services and activities rated – in terms of market shares, market opinions, etc.

6 What will be the most effective *distribution* channels?

7 What will be the most effective *communication* channels?

Summary

Think of advertising, promotion, merchandising – in fact all internal and external 'messages' as *communication*.

Review this communication – content and methods – constantly:

- What are we saying?

- How are we saying it?

- Where are we saying it?

- When are we saying it?

Remember that, in today's 'clutter', you need to grab people's attention:
- Gain   reader/viewer/listener *interest*.

- Build on *benefits* to fulfil *needs/desires*.

- Encourage   *action*;   invite people to participate or make a decision.

- Do not try to say too much.

- This is the era of one-to-one communication – capitalise wherever possible on such techniques. Use personalised approaches – utilise computer listings of prime prospects – then follow up with interesting, regular mailings.

- Do not underestimate the value of good, old-fashioned words; do not try to be too smart. People are still attracted to phrases including 'free', 'hurry', 'special' and the like.

Avoid overkill. For example, with direct-mail campaigns such as letter-box drops, check how/when/where with the distribution contractor. It is fast reaching the stage where, some days, a householder needs a wheelbarrow to cart the circulars from the top of the drive.

10

Public relations – huckster's craft or communication aid?

Like advertising, public relations is viewed by many as an unjustifiable intrusion.

Consider, though, the real role of public relations: 'The art and science of planning and implementing honest, two-way communication and understanding between a company and the many groups, with which it is concerned in the course of its various operations.'

The aims of a campaign for improved public relations (or public affairs or corporate affairs) can be many and varied. Good, sound public relations can foster effective and widespread coverage by the media to explain a company's services, products and, in many cases, its 'non-business' activities as well.

Ideally, a company should strive to achieve a situation whereby the media contacts that company for pertinent remarks on matters of public interest. Your image is greatly improved when you are quoted as the spokesperson or authority on matters related to your business sphere.

Public relations goes beyond media releases

Profile-building and heightened public awareness are only one aspect of public relations. Others are: to cement the relationship between say, your company and your distributors; or to build morale among your own staff. Being connected with a newsworthy (in the positive sense) company gives a warm glow to your people. The 'good place to work/far-sighted employer' label can also boost your recruitment programmes.

Do-it-yourself benefits

Advantages of an in-house public relations system, as opposed to relying totally on outside specialists, are numerous. Media personnel react far more favourably to material sources from a principal than an intermediary. The news is then available 'straight from the horse's mouth'.

Business people frequently ask, 'How do we maintain a flow of news?' It is simple. For most organisations, a release 'calendar' can be plotted to act as a checklist for monthly reviews. Annual or biannual results, new product developments, overseas achievements, expansion programmes –there is a world of news waiting to be devoured not only by the general media at large but also by specialists and trade publications.

By developing your own profile-building exercise, you are enhancing the believability factor, controlling the content of your news releases, and reducing the chances of misinterpretation. Cost benefits apply too.

Do not forget, this matter of public relations extends within an organisation. In-house newsletters, bulletins, staff functions to update your people – all these are grist to the mill of public relations.

Public relations extends beyond capitalising on written or broadcast opportunities. Speaking engagements, presentations at conferences and seminars, participation in trade events, sponsorships – these are just a handful of vehicles that need to be scrutinised and evaluated by astute marketers.

Video extends horizons

And, if it is true that a single picture speaks a thousand words, do not overlook the video revolution. Video and other audio-visual aids can be used to 'demonstrate' your achievements, and to promulgate your messages to internal staff, agents, distributors or media.

As with pocket calculators, video gear has come of age in terms of portability. Costwise, it does not break the bank – alternatively, one can hire equipment and production expertise on an hourly basis.

The value of video extends way beyond the domain of public relations. In-house training, safety procedures, new product specifications, sales programme instructions – all these and much more relate to public relations if we bear in mind some of those key words in the opening definition: planning two-way communication. That is what good, believable, honest 'communications relations' with your many publics should be concerned with.

Summary

- Use public relations to achieve honest, open, two-way communication.

- Aim your public relations not only at the media but also at your own people, stockists, agents and other intermediaries.

- Editorial comment is far more believable than bought advertising space.

- A sound programme of public or corporate relations can foster much goodwill, internally as well as externally.

- Familiarise yourself with the assorted communication devices essential to convey public relations messages.

- Do not be misled into thinking that success with public relations means hiring a 'whizz, bang, big bucks' consultancy.

11
Point-of-sale pointers

In terms of invested pounds, the amount of money that is spent in helping to move merchandise off shelves today is staggering. So manufacturers should ensure that point-of-sale material plays an active role in the goods-movement machinery. Impact gained at the point of purchase can make – or break – a sale.

The same can be said of packaging or labelling. If these things let you down, your customer can change his or her mind and the sale is killed – despite the fact that the product measures up to its promise, the advertising played a useful role, and the price was competitively set.

'Point of sale' refers to the support material with the goods at the place where the product is located. Very often, this is the last 'promoter' before our consumer takes the product.

Critics may argue that point-of-sale application is limited to day-to-day items, impulse-purchase goods, and so on. This is untrue. Let us examine consumer durables. Some would say that the decision is already made when the consumer moves to actually buy. After all, a major outlay for items such as refrigerators, colour televisions or motor vehicles is generally coupled with careful pre-planning. But what about the 'floating' market – those potential customers who are 'just browsing thanks'?

People look around

It is fair to remark that as often as not a degree of 'window shopping' precedes the shopper's final decision.

Moving back to our less costly, 'everyday' items, a supermarket parallel provides the best illustration. With the advent of self-selection, it has become imperative that point-of-sale material – whether it be a pack design or poster or display unit – is properly taken into consideration and its application thought through as an integral element of the whole approach to marketing your wares.

Supermarkets provide a challenge to modern marketers and those with product responsibilities. A great brain once said, 'Products multiply and the mind subtracts.' In other words, competition is very fierce, many manufacturers are competing for a share of what customers spend, and products are often not measurably different. So, in addition to the promise, the quality, the price/value, and so on, that last effort at the place of purchase can significantly influence your share of the market.

Retail calls for distinct skills

If you rely on supermarkets – or, for that matter, on any retail outlet – as part of your distribution chain, maximise opportunities. Put yourself in the customer's position. What catches your eye when you walk in? Where are the in-store locations that hold prime appeal? Seek new and attractive ways to display your wares – and do not neglect the stockist. Find out what key stockists expect, and what they will accommodate. Then get to work. Gondola ends, bins, mobiles, shelf strips – all have their place. Think beyond posters and placards.

Stress the importance of full shelves and clean stock with your representatives – better still, if you can afford it, start to think about merchandise detailers. Make sure that forward stocks are prominent, and that back-up stock is available.

Link your promotion

Too often an advertising mix thoroughly scrutinises the major elements – television, newspapers, magazines and radio – yet neglects the final merchandising links. To maximise value from your advertising investment, learn to place yourself in the end-user's role. Is there a case for mailing a price-off or discount offer? What will appeal to the decision-maker?

Think through the steps our typical shopper takes before the hand reaches out to the shelf: he or she draws up a shopping list, scans specials in the newspaper, and maybe looks at or hears advertisements for the product. Yet all his or her work – and that of the advertisers – can disappear in a flash at the last moment when the product is handled before being placed into a shopping trundler.

Impulse purchase do not escape; nor do low-cost items. That is where you should aim for repeat business more aggressively. Think about ways to introduce trial-sampling, either by trial packs or in-store promotion (e.g., taste trials for food/drink products). This is rather important if you are following someone else to market . . . and do not want to be labelled as just another 'me too' product.

What price, then, brand loyalty if you are missing out at the final point? That is where the impulse decision can switch selection very quickly. True, people may be inclined to buy some items solely on price – but it is rarely the be all and end all.

Big-ticket items need back-up

In some ways, it may be easier, and less cut-throat, with the major items we covered towards the beginning. Or is it? The stakes are greater, and impulse inclinations are less significant. That gives you more opportunity to win at the point of purchase – perhaps even to gain the switch from a competitor. For our 'just looking thanks' horde, provide literature – something they can take away, browse through, and read. It may firm up their mind to buy your product. It is the retailers' job to get those people back into their stores. But manufacturers can help, and also win kudos, if they allow for an address panel on literature – or, better still, if they overprint or overstamp the stockists' details.

With both day-to-day products and high-cost goods, appearance and support elements at the point of sale require constant attention and improvement. Do you want the stockists to motivate the customer for you? Then motivate the stockists! Give them the items they need to build their store traffic. You provide the ammunition; they load and fire – it is as simple as that. If you win the stockists, you are almost there – you can start to push for prime showroom or window space and a greater area for your display items.

The size of your operation is no deterrent. Big manufacturers may have more resources, but this does not mean that they are the only ones to think creatively. Small concerns can readily train their representatives to carry merchandising gear and co-operate with stockists. Give represent-atives display guides and kits; possibly offer them incentives – perhaps a competition for the best display, with prizes for the representative and the stockist.

In short, we are all permitted to use our imagination. If you do this, and pay attention to the point of purchase/point of sale, you will be able to look forward to happy stockists and satisfied customers – which, after all is said and done, helps add up to an increased market share, which is so often a step towards more profitable marketing.

Summary

- 'Silent' displays and aids are an integral part of the sales arsenal.

- Learn what catches shoppers' attention.

- Find out what the stockist needs to ensure that you gain improved displays.

- The entire promotion effort should be linked. Themes and promises in media advertising campaigns should be carried through to posters, banners and merchandising material. A reinforced message has greater memorability.

12

Electronic media and marketing plans

The new television and radio developments that have hit the airwaves in recent years can, properly organised and properly controlled, be beneficial for viewers, listeners and advertisers alike.

As far as impact and advertising costs are concerned, television is the medium that attracts the most involved attention. We have had steam radio around for a long time now, and it is a well-proved medium. Any improvements there merely add lustre to an already well-designed advertising tool.

It is in the field of television that the headaches emerge. If agencies want to maintain and increase their clients' level of spending, they may need to pay more attention to planning advertising campaigns. After all, from an agency's stance, it is a great advantage to have bountiful television billings – that is where the big money lies.

Colour is life

To maintain perspective, it is necessary to remember that colour has made a tremendous impact on television.

Television has transformed almost every aspect of our lives. It has great strengths over print and radio. Television combines sight and sound; it demonstrates products; it brings events into our homes as they happen. It is alive.

From the advertisers' point of view, television can provide believability more capably than anything else, short of actually sampling and approving the product.

With the current welter of advertising messages, it becomes increasingly difficult for the consumer to avoid exhortations to buy this and buy that. This in turn creates new obstacles for advertisers, who must endeavour to ensure that their messages are absorbed.

One report claims that, on average, the brain is expected to store up to 600 messages per day – though, admittedly, they are not all commercially inclined. Nevertheless, if you ponder how many things you were told, heard, read or saw in one average day, the list would be far more extensive than you probably envisaged.

As a result, we have become accustomed to absorbing images in a split second. Often, the subconscious will note and file a message for future reference use. Even people who say, 'I hate the commercial for XYZ product', are at least *noticing* the message.

With the advent of colour, television as an advertising medium gained five major strengths:

- **Increased attention value:** Colour will catch the eye where black and white fail.

- **Realism:** With many products (and the same can be said of actual film programmes) colour is important in display or presentation. It helps to depict goods in the manner in which the human eye is accustomed to viewing them.

- **Identity:** It is very important to remember that colours are more easily retained in the memory than words or symbols. Used to identify a product or service and persistently employed to build up recognition, colour has an extremely powerful influence.

- **Psychology:** Because of the many mental and emotional effects of colour, subtle applications are possible. Colours can imply warmth, coolness, cleanliness, etc. They can be extremely effective in helping lead the consumer into an 'I want to buy' situation. Think of the seasonal connotations for products such as refrigerators and freezers, promoted during summer, or tropical island holidays, advertised in mid-winter.

- **Beauty:** Colour possesses intrinsic appeal. Clarified in drawing or photography, it will create heightened interest and can have a direct bearing on the message being broadcast, making it extremely effective. Colour alone has, in some instances, through cleverness and strategy, produced some of the best advertisements ever composed.

The five preceding points are not original. However, they need to be borne in mind, especially with the high number of channels encountered in many developed countries.

There are ground rules to follow, and provided both clients and agencies do their homework properly, the system creates minimum discomfort for all concerned.

A carefully planned approach

Let us look at some other influences on marketing in a modern broadcasting environment.

Ratings are television's life-blood. There are no great fears with only two or three channels. A media planner's nightmare occurs when the number swells and you add cable or satellite television.

With several channels competing for viewers, the *programming* is more crucial than in single-channel situations. In turn, advertisers will want to ensure that their commercials are slotted in when the *audience figures* are at their best. So more attention must be paid by agencies to finding out what's on air, when it is screening, and likely audience levels.

The right approach to setting television *advertising budgets* is important. Some advertisers, on account of their products and the target markets they appeal to, find it necessary to invest larger sums overall in order to maintain desired awareness, particularly in those cases where the audiences are approaching significant levels for competing channels.

Sponsorship is still in its infancy. Some of the big spenders on television may have budgets sufficiently large to afford sponsorship of special programmes or series if or when this aspect of communication reaches a level comparable to that of the United States.

Advertising agencies will need to perform

All in all, there is going to be a great deal more attention to winning billings – and keeping them. After all, advertisers have supposedly known for years that the people they have been talking to in their commercials are not idiots. Some of the basic guidelines set for customers must rub off on the advertisers! Soon they will be in the position most of their publics are in – that of making a rational choice between alternative offerings.

So advertisers will have to learn to ask more questions of their agencies and of the sources from which they are buying air time. Agencies in turn will have to gear themselves up to talking in sensible terms about reach and frequency.

We now see the networks and radio stations advertising in order to win viewers and listeners. Just as the audiences are going to get a whole lot smarter, so too will advertisers be required to watch more closely how far their air-time spend goes when it is spread across a variety of channels or radio stations.

And spare a thought for the poor old end-user. Now we are faced with a double decision: not just which brand to buy, but which channel or station to tell us which brand to buy.

13

Service – the Cinderella of marketing

When people define marketing, 'profit' is frequently overlooked. By the same token, 'service' and 'after-sales service' tend to be downplayed in some marketing mixes. It is the more visible 'glamour' elements, such as selling and promotion, that hog the limelight.

Those of us who seek to build a successful business – one to which our customers will return to make further purchases – should scrutinise our follow-up service and after-sales service.

After-sales service is not something peculiar to the motor vehicle industry. And, speaking of motor vehicles, the service element should be called to mind every time we pull into a service station. Come to think of it, why are they called service stations? Rarely does one enjoy the privilege of an attendant offering to check oil, water, tyres; with increasing frequency, we are expected to fill our own petrol tanks.

We are after repeat business

Service and post-sales service in marketing focus on cementing the repeat-business/ongoing-customer-relationship link. They deal with numerous processes, systems or benefits aimed at simplifying or enhancing our offers. These can include things such as credit facilities and payment methods, follow-up to check satisfaction, the rectification of any faults, the ability to deliver on time, quality assurance and quality control, and ease of purchase or transaction completion.

These things are often so simple that they are dismissed as unnecessary. However, many suppliers are, providing similar (sometimes the same) goods and services. They are all making the same promises. What happens? The buyer, whether housewife or purchasing officer, is looking for that 'edge of difference', the extra something. And as we have already stated, things like brand loyalty are largely outdated. Today's buyer is not a moron – he or she seeks value for money.

Beyond price

Now here is the twist: because value for money goes way beyond the price tag, after-sales service, quality, reliability, etc. are essential for success.

Too many trading organisations have abandoned the basic yet important criteria by which they are judged. These same organisations will go to great and expensive lengths to promote aggressively, mount sophisticated advertising campaigns, and employ supposedly professional salespeople. Sadly, however, they fail to use their business imagination sufficiently in order to look beyond satisfying the immediate need.

To such people, long-term planning is a silly buzz-phrase; lateral thinking probably has something to do with pruning fruit trees; and as for being market as opposed to product oriented . . . suggest such corporate blasphemy and you'll encounter their stock 'We've always done it this way' dismissal.

The old ways no longer work

For several decades, there was no real need to market. Old habits die hard – especially with producer boards and government departments and long-established business pioneers. Suddenly they need to face up to some rather sticky facts of economic life. Many individuals and nations alike are squirming because they are living beyond their means. Politicians rave about light at the end of tunnels. In the meantime, interest rates, inflation and exchange rates still hiccup merrily. What the situation boils down to is this: many countries need lots of the things that overseas countries produce; but those overseas countries, in turn, do not necessarily need what their customer countries produce.

Take sheep meat, once a big money-earner for New Zealand. Dealing with Iran, a nation that displays an on-again-off-again, wait-and-see meat-buying approach, coupled with a barter system for eventually settling long-standing debts, has rather frightening overtones. And, with reducing oil prices, the Iranian side of the barter could also be devaluing.

Such is the risk when you put too many of your trading eggs – or sheep carcasses – in one basket. After-sales service is the type of aid that alerts us to dwindling or volatile markets, permitting the development of alternative, replacement marketing strategies.

Added value, high quality, realistic pricing, and exemplary service – these are some of the considerations that assure success in today's highly volatile global and local market-places. Note how we need to move far beyond pricing – in fact, this chapter should probably be read in conjunction with the points made in Chapter 5.

Domino effect

The requirement for excellent service and follow-up has increased in proportion to the reduction in apathy by modern consumers. Our forefathers accepted third-rate service; they stuck with brands, banks, lawyers and laundry products. It was the done thing.

This no longer happens. People fight back. We could all probably relate a host of situations where we have received a less-than-acceptable degree of service or after-sales attention. Some personal instances involve:

- An expensive electronic typewriter: the first model was faulty and eventually replaced. Ongoing faults continued. Unpleasant discussions over the service contract took place. We enquired about changing the model – a ludicrous trade-in price was offered.

- One of the biggest national motor vehicle chains: eight cars (that is the biggest proportion of a lifetime ownership) had been purchased from or serviced by members of that group over 24 years – until the last one, which was the proverbial pup.

- A chartered accountant, senior partner in a leading practice: sent a bill for talking to us on the telephone to check why we had written saying the practice's services were no longer required.

- Spa-pool and spa-pool filter companies: it was great to discover that warranties are not worth the paper they are written on when parts start malfunctioning.

- Insurance companies: it was quite a different story to the one given when signing-up when claim or pay-out time came around.

But we do learn our lessons, like switching after 23 years with the same bank, which had handled business and personal accounts, as well as family's accounts – small potatoes compared with big corporate customers no doubt. Nevertheless, there were loans, investments, savings accounts, cheque accounts and credit cards but our business and loyalty were apparently of little importance. We had even used their correspondent banks in other parts of the world. You know, the decision to switch is one we have never regretted. It should have been done at least ten years earlier.

The real moral of the story, though, is that whenever friends or business associates ask about things like electronic office equipment, private vehicles, business fleets, personal insurance, company superannuation funds, spa pools, accountants, or banks – we simply say, 'Well, here's who we *would not* deal with, ———. . . .'

A generation later, young adults are not so easily trampled on. This is the age of working wives, dual incomes, and people who are not afraid to assert themselves.

In turn, service and after-sales service must be superb. Marketing promises need to be commercial facts, not fiction.

Examples

A high-technology company supplying specialist products to manufacturers: 17 per cent of respondents reported that pricing was the most important factor influencing purchasing decisions. The majority (83 per cent) of respondents stressed:

- reliability
- co-operation
- quality
- delivery
- follow-up
- understanding the customer's needs.

Factors measured for a consumer product range marketed nationally through retail chemists' shops resulted in the following 'service ahead of price only' findings – listed in order of importance:

- high fashion
- media advertising support
- wide selection of styles
- price
- quality.

For an international company, we determined the importance of factors among 'trade' respondents. In general, these respondents were purchasing executives with large manufacturing or processing organisations: 12 per cent of the sample mentioned price as the most important factor.

The remaining 88 per cent of the sample ranked factors in the following order:

- continuity of product supply and reliability
- product quality
- service and back-up.

14

Choose your target

Segmentation, niche marketing, target marketing – they all spotlight the same thing: a careful, selective approach to business activities designed to capitalise on strengths.

The ability to pin-point where your marketing effort, or activities such as selling or promotion, should be concentrated must be constantly honed. The 'targeting' approach can pay off handsomely through increased productivity and profitability. Less waste – of money, time, materials, effort and personnel – is the outcome.

Market segments

Thinking about our market in terms of segments rather than as a whole permits us to identify the levels of support and service required in relation to potential and profit. As time progresses, it becomes possible to ascertain with a high degree of accuracy whether specific segments are rising, static or declining. Efforts can then be weighted accordingly.

Apart from market segments, there are numerous other areas that can be established as targets to home in on. These include:

- Product segments.
- Geographical segments (local and overseas markets).
- Direct segments (reached through your own efforts).
- Indirect segments (where an intermediary is employed to 'sell on' to your end-users).
- Customer segments.

Do not overlook consumer and industry segments – all buyers cannot be treated in the same manner. Consumers, for example, may be young, old, married, single, well-off, not-so-well-off, and so on. And what about ethnic segments? Different cultures have different backgrounds, interpretations and requirements.

Each segment applicable to your business sphere should be methodically assembled; each must be reviewed as a distinct market or a separate public.

Segmentation/targeting reduces costs

Some critics might argue that the 'unit' cost of developing targeted programmes is relatively higher than that in a blanket approach. Not so. In the long run, cost efficiencies must emerge through concentrating on the best opportunities and avoiding waste.

The selective-marketing technique isolates lucrative bases. Naturally, as with most things, there are exceptions. Some general-purpose, widely used products may be exceptions. Mind you, if one of these products were provided by a number of suppliers, target marketing could still become the order of the day to create an edge of excellence and specific appeal.

Small businesses, especially, can avoid vulnerability if they accept this segment-target principle. It works hand in hand with positioning – deciding what business you are in, and what your main aims are, before setting out to be the very best in your field. One person working from a basement underneath their home is not precluded from being the best at his or her craft. . . .

Determining opportunities

Opportunities for specialisation can be isolated through the targeted approach. Specialisation can mean an outstanding advance for a small business. Specialisation does not automatically translate as unique – again, decide what business you are really in, define what you do best, and concentrate on that instead of trying to be all things to all customers. Resist the temptation to rush madly all over the place dabbling in this, that, and the other business activity.

For the not-so-large company, small can be beautiful. Small companies can be faster on their feet than their heavyweight competitors. Points can be scored against the bigger opposition, because the little fellow is geared to smaller runs and smaller orders. A midget-size company can provide a far more personal service than the Goliath trader.

Small companies should target carefully

What the small company lacks in resources – such as hordes of people and oodles of money – can be compensated for by careful planning that seeks to uncover those profitable niches.

Target marketing, when all is said and done, comes back to using a disciplined planning system to know where you should be concentrating your effort and how to best husband your resources.

Currently, it is in vogue to talk about entrepreneurial flair and to put this up as the magic ingredient for real success. True, entrepreneurial flair and a creative approach to business are essential. But they need to be tempered with the planned, systematic approach.

Sir Freddie Laker, the British businessman who set the travel world reeling with his approach to trans-Atlantic airline marketing in the 1970s put the targeted, planned system into perspective. In early 1982, after the demise of his empire, he said: 'For 33 years I got it right, but in the thirty-fourth year I got it wrong.'

In the absence of a crystal ball, tread carefully up a *selected* path to reduce the chances of 'getting it wrong'.

Summary

- Pin-point your marketing effort to capitalise on the most lucrative customers and areas.

- Small and large organisations alike must realise that a market comprises several 'parts'. Select those parts that best suit your type of business and your resources.

- Segmentation and targeting reduce waste, saving time, money and energy.

- Segmentation is firing a rifle – not discharging a shotgun.

15

A blueprint for survival – written plans

On the first Tuesday of each November the Australasian workforce grinds to a halt. That is the day on which the Melbourne Cup, one of the world's richest horse-races, is run. As with any gambling, some of the punters win, some of the punters lose. So what?

Now, a flutter on the ponies is one thing, but to gamble or punt recklessly in business is another. We are not talking about playing around with stocks and shares; we are talking about people who take foolhardy business risks – people who jeopardise the success of their business operation.

We can – and should – eliminate as much risk as possible, by paying more attention to forward planning. But the majority of small (and many medium-sized) businesses do not operate with a written plan – a plan that sets out where they are heading in the long term.

Far too many people shelter behind a smoke-screen by proclaiming (as they point to their heads), 'We don't need a written plan – we carry it all up here.' Then they walk out of the office and get run over by a bus.

Earlier in this book, when we were discussing communication, we mentioned the enormous number of messages that we are expected to store in our minds and the fact that most of what we hear is forgotten within a day. Surely this risk of *forgetting* highlights the need to write things down.

If you do not have a plan, how do you know where you are going? Without objectives (where do we want to get to?) and strategies (how are we going to get there?) tied into a time frame, where is the course to plot a company's direction?

As soon as we have posed questions, we need to provide answers – record them, albeit briefly and succinctly, in a planning document. Questions are the very essence of planning. And, without disciplined planning, you are courting disaster.

Marketers need to know where their business has been coming from, where it is currently, and where it will be coming from in future. Theirs and their competitors' market shares and activities need to be scrutinised and projected. They must be aware not only of overall performance but also of performance by product, service, area, territory, industry segment or consumer classification. It is important to note whether performance and results are ahead, behind or static related to value and volume predictions.

That is the mere tip of the marketing-plan iceberg. Excellent texts and guides are readily available on how to prepare useful, functional marketing plans. Our aim is simply to alert readers to the need to plan in a disciplined, step-by-step manner; guideline headings are included at the end of this chapter.

Crystal-ball gazing

Discipline must embody a forward-looking philosophy. Where do we want to be in, say, five years? Set the *long-term aims*, then work backwards so that current goals are relevant to the broader corporate fabric.

Do not bleat about plans adding to the paper war. For the majority of companies, plans need not be cumbersome, hefty documents. Rather, they are *working* guides to be *used* and *reviewed*. They are not carved from tablets of stone either. Just as the market place and other sections of the trading environment are subject to shifts and changes, so too is any plan a flexible document.

There are many alternatives for plan styles. Some folk use check-lists, others flow charts. Develop a style or format to suit your specific needs – and ensure that it covers all the aspects relevant to *your* business.

Relevance means planning must not be a reclusive or isolated activity. Good, sound planning involves people from various sections and levels of the company. Certainly, someone has to make the final decisions. Before you reach that stage, however, encourage and obtain inputs from your key people, ensuring that all sections contribute openly.

Synergy, harmony, integration

The workable scheme of things advocated reaches beyond marketing. The integration of all plans covering all aspects or primary functions of the business is essential to success.

Our 'series of plans' could well start with a company plan (corporate goals, future directions). This plan dictates to the sectional plans, which, after all, must support the company's overall strategy.

That support needs to be spelled out in sectional plans, which, depending on your business, could well set out directions, actions and timing in connection with:

- Marketing.
- Manufacturing.
- Finance.
- Personnel.

These are the *broad* headings to cover our key probes:

- What does the market want?
- Can we make it?
- Will it be profitable?
- Do we have, or can we recruit and train, the necessary people?

This is simplistic, but it is a start.

Each key plan 'subdivides' into pertinent, applicable sections. For example, the marketing plan may well include:

- Product plans.
- Market plans.
- Sales plans.
- Advertising and promotion plans.

or, at the very least, objectives and strategies relevant to the main marketing elements.

Importantly, by avoiding a slack approach to planning, and ensuring synergy, a business works as a total unit – not a fragmented series of poorly co-ordinated functions.

All too often we hear the mournful cry from senior management, 'I have to spend too much time putting out bush fires.' Much of this fire-fighting would be avoided if companies spent a little more time organising themselves and attending to forward planning.

Systematic analysis that establishes aims and goals and specifies how to accomplish those aims and goals at the lowest possible cost just has to trump taking a punt. Planning may not eliminate risk, but it certainly helps us to reduce uncertainty. As already mentioned, it forces us to check where we are headed.

By reducing the element of uncertainty, resources can be organised to meet changing circumstances with an improved degree of confidence –or, as the business vernacular of the day puts it, to read the warning signs before the manure hits the fan.

Each year, some new American or British business book emerges as a best seller. Such books are worth reading – providing they are kept in perspective. For many business people, the experiences, examples, solutions or case studies spawned in the mega-markets are not realistic.

Size, corporate muscle and budgets create a dimension that may be suited to the 'Top 10' but is of little relevance to the mainstream, medium-scale operations that comprise the overwhelming majority of businesses.

The answer is to learn from the 'biggies', but keep your own approach simple. For simplicity in planning, my favourite checklist does not come from a textbook. It is that journalist's maxim penned by Rudyard Kipling:

> I keep six honest serving-men
> They taught me all I knew;
> Their names are *What* and *Why* and *When*
> And *How* and *Where* and *Who*.

Those six key words provide an excellent, easily remembered basis for planning. And planning should, in turn, be built around a framework based on our specific real-time situation. Overall goals must be established; they will be reached by harnessing total resources and recognising financial, marketing, production and personnel strengths, as well as weaknesses.

Products, services, money, people, support, administration – it does not take long to assemble a list of pertinent criteria. The secret of survival is to be able to write the answers – even if they are guesstimates –alongside each key point.

Plans are there to be used

Throughout this chapter, we have argued that plans are vital, living items to be used as part of one's day-to-day approach to running a successful business. As such, they act as control guides.

Once established as such a guide, plans allow you to extract a list of priorities. In setting out items requiring attention and action, include what must be done, who is to do it, and the deadline for each task's completion.

With such an approach, each section of a business is co-ordinated, employees and management have a clearer vision of directions, and the risk of 'forgetting to do something' is reduced.

When we reviewed the place of research in the marketing mix, that element's orientation towards customers or external forces was stressed. This is also true with planning. Do not make assumptions or judgements based only on gut feelings.

For many, an adaption of marketing audit principles provides a sensible foundation for planning. As opposed to financial audits (which tend to look back at historical events), marketing audits are an extremely positive device. Essentially, they are an independent, systematic and critical look at the entire marketing effort made by a company or industry.

Marketing audits review activities and situations; they determine what is being carried out; they evaluate activities; and, where pertinent, they recommend what should be done. They provide a positive, constructive approach based on external (market) as well as internal factors.

This same principle of evaluation before commitment applies beyond marketing. Sadly, human nature makes most of us wait until we are feeling the pinch before we ask, 'What's wrong with the way we are running our business?'

An audit, or review, should be an ongoing exercise, not a crisis-inspired event. It need not rely on outside specialists, although the objectivity of independent people not caught up in the everyday detail is an advantage.

Whatever happens, look critically at activities; plan to capitalise on opportunities, stifle threats, and combat weaknesses. And, above all else, do not *think* about such things – commit those thoughts to paper.

Example

To demonstrate how marketing planning has an impact beyond market-ing: in 1983 a consultant was briefed to review a major public company's approach to marketing. The client's main product arena to be examined centred around rigid packaging materials.

As part of a group of companies, the interrelationship between the specific client and other divisions had to be considered, together with assorted decentralised regional manufacturing operations. Recommend-ations were also required to strengthen the company's export activities.

A marketing audit was conducted to review the division's entire operations, including its head office, regional locations, and specialist operating subsidiaries. This enabled pertinent, workable and achievable short- and long-term recommendations to be prepared.

The marketing approach was developed to heed the company's industrial and technical profile, along with the impact of direct and indirect, local and foreign competition.

Priorities were established and a time frame calculated. A detailed one-year marketing plan and a more general five-year strategy plan were put in place.

Planning covered information systems, forward regional evaluations, and product adjustments, plus segmentation by key industries to produce better sales and development deployment.

The roles of and weighting for all marketing elements, matched to the company's special needs and product variations, were detailed.

The brief's parameters were extended as the project progressed. It became obvious that an organisational and structural 'rethink' would be required; a marketing section would need to be put in place, but it would need to avoid duplication of line activities already operating within and beyond the division under scrutiny.

Once a structure had been concluded, advice centred on the recruitment and appointment of a marketing manager and marketing assistants. Job descriptions were prepared, and, in the longer term, an opportunity emerged to combine two major divisions under a single marketing 'umbrella' – creating considerable savings for the company, along with a far more complementary product mix.

The golden rule is:

- Plan.
- Measure.
- Re-examine.
- Remain flexible.

Checklist: how to extract background for a marketing plan

1 **Markets:**
Total market size, our share; potential.
Market – and specific segments – growing or declining.
Factors that affect our market.
Market profiles: geographical; industry types (customers); referrals and intermediaries.
Direct competition.
Indirect competition.
Regional 'pictures' and their differing requirements.
Seasonal or cyclical trends.
Market changes – past/future.
Services and products – past/future.
Demand trends – past/future.

2 **Products and services:**
Major users, by product/service – translate as industry groups/segments.
Relate to competitors' products/services and *their* major users.
Relate to market place needs.
Unique qualities or benefits.
Pluses – price, product, service, etc.
Strengths and weaknesses.
Proposed changes related to market-place dictates.
Existing products/services' images.
Image for any proposed products/services.
New introductions – launch, trial, monitoring, timing; adjustments – wider release.
Pre-introduction of new developments – educate, train,

check test marketing, pilot programmes.

Any culling of products or modifications to existing ones.

3   **Price:**

Our pricing versus competitors'.

Any special activities conducted by competitors (bulk dealings, volume business, etc.)?

Importance of price variations for commodities versus higher technology/specialist items; leader, follower, opportunity costing, quantitative discounts.

4   **Distribution:**

Effectiveness of current methods – freighting, stockholding.

Competitors' distribution methods.

Alternatives.

Intermediaries' strengths/ weaknesses.

Percentage of business via intermediaries.

5   **Selling:**

Sales budgets and targets – by area, by product or service grouping.

Selling force – type, location.

Sales training – induction and regular, ongoing training.

Field supervision.

Internal sales liaison and back-up.

Product/service knowledge; skills and specialist strengths; cross-sell range or separate detailing?

Sales analysis and systems to provide marketing planning information.

Existing salespeople able to handle new services or special projects without diluting current efforts?

Sufficient personnel – number, calibre?

Sales support material, aids (extending to intermediaries' requirements).

Physical and non-physical selling (mail, direct response, reminder systems, etc.).

Sales cycles, levels of service, special 'drives'.

6   **Advertising, promotion and public relations:**

Communication objectives.

Media and non-media advertising.

Advertising 'promises' – what to say, where to say.

Action/enquiry-oriented?

Yours versus competitors' spending, promises, activities.

Corporate and product/service programmes.

Area requirements – regional support.

Linked communication – to improve image and recall, to reduce cost and increase effectiveness of communication.

Editorial activities versus 'bought' space.

Briefing methods – outside agencies to achieve creative

excellence and cost effectiveness.

Media selection – evaluate.

Below-line activities – evaluate merchandising, point-of-sale material.

In-house developments – using own resources.

Literature – promotional and 'news' content.

Packaging, shippers, display units.

Pre- and post-test material.

Displays/merchandising – static and 'live' functions.

Internal promotion/communication to advise proposals – including attention to intermediaries and referrals.

7 **Competition in the market place:**
Similar products and services.
Indirect competition.
Competitors' reputations, performance, methods, locations, international links, reach.
Changes introduced or planned by competitors.
Competitors' market shares.
Personnel ability, training, remuneration schemes.
Image, advertising, promotion.
Expenditure – how much, where spent.

8 **Economic and demographic factors:**
Money, inflation.
Industry trends, shifts.
Population spread.

9 **Supply factors:**
Materials.
Equipment.

10 **Legal factors:**
Regulations or restrictions, forward changes.
Domestic and export market places.

11 **Sundry variables:**
Production capacity.
Manufacturing.
Unions.

12 **Social factors:**
Changing life-style.
Working wives.
Dual-income families.
Increased leisure time.

13 **Customers' attitudes:**
What influences decisions?
Who influences?
Frequency of purchase.
Loyalty.
Perceived strengths/weaknesses of ourselves and competitors.

14 **Marketing research:**
Existing information and internal material.
Methods – desk, field, own resources, outside requirements.
Marketing intelligence – informal and formal feedback.

15 **Budget setting:**
Historical, percentage, zero-base or task method.
Value, units, kilograms, people, products and time.

Area amounts – area activities. Training, conferences and 'people' support.

16 **Integration:**
Marketing plan – tie in with manufacturing, financial and personnel planning.

17 **Schedule:**
Main items emerging, action priorities, allocation of responsibilities, deadlines and time frame.

Summary

- Define the *business* we are in.

- Set out *corporate objectives* and goals, defined to determine the standards required.

- Devise the corporate *strategies* – the course of action necessary to achieve the targets set.

- Ensure the best use of your *money*, *products*, *services*, *knowledge*, *skills* and *people* resources.

- Devise the *tactics* – details and specific responsibilities and tasks.

- Ensure that a *monitoring* system is built in to allow periodic reviews and adjustments.

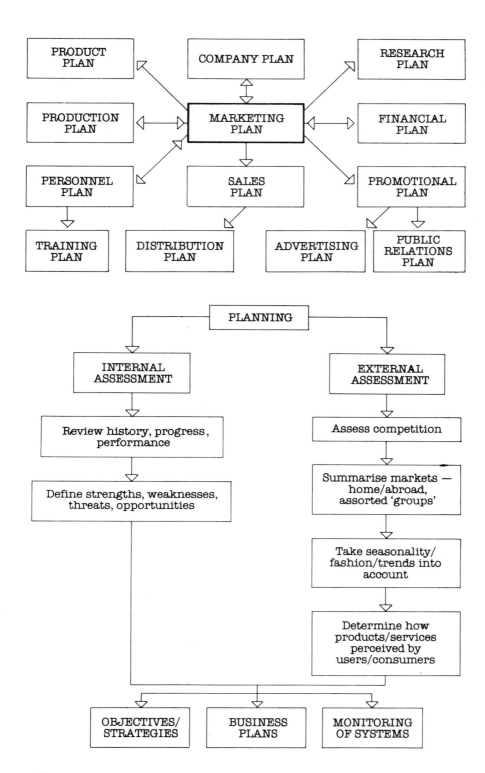

Figure 4

16

Do not count on gut feeling

Far too many companies claim, 'We can sort out our own marketing', yet they still have not grasped the basic principles of marketing. It would be interesting – or should we say frightening? – to estimate the cost of wasted expenditure in areas of product or service introduction, advertising, distribution and sales through brushing aside the need for marketing and sticking to a 'We think this is the best way; we've always done it like this' attitude.

Sadly, a number of companies just do not want to know about marketing in its proper sense. At best, it is a description to cover their selling structure, to cloud it in a mystique designed to impress competitors. It sounds much better to call a good field performer a 'marketing representative' or an area sales manager 'marketing manager' than plain 'salesperson' or 'sales manager' (not that we are for one moment knocking salespeople – far from it).

Some of our leaders in industry need to gain a much clearer perspective, to separate the roles and establish a distinct place for each specialist activity in the wider marketing context.

You can shuck off the stock-in-trade jargon of some marketers and very quickly get down to basics such as 'What does the customer need?' Too many people *think* they know what the customer/consumer needs. Do not just give him or her what he or she wants or else you will be putting some very costly, low-quantity runs through production lines. If mass production leading to mass consumption is the answer to keeping prices for goods stable and reasonable, then is it not fair to assume that the first commandment must be 'Know thy market'?

Sensible, basic, proven steps

Ground-roots marketing – and this applies whether you are manufacturing goods (consumer durables/consumer perishables sounds more pontifical) or promoting services – has an application in almost every instance. The food processer who wants to be first into the market place with some new line; the bank that wonders about a new savings scheme to attract more depositors; the motel proprietor considering the instalment of video for his or her guests – all are involved in some form of marketing, even if it is rather elementary.

In most cases, we can isolate the essential steps of a sensible, rudimentary approach to marketing and apply them across the board. Obviously, applications vary depending on your line of business . . . no problem. Select the applicable stages. Ask yourself if you are doing these things. If you are, then think about improvement, forward planning, and future trends. If you are not, then it is time you were.

Tell people about your product. Tell them in believable terms. (Perhaps at this point you get back to research: How do we talk to them? Where do we attract their attention? Creative direction can be superb; choosing the wrong media can be fatal, no matter how appealing the pictures and words.)

Salespeople (yes, there is just as much need for internal promotion or public relations as external) must be educated first. If they do not believe that smoked eel goes with cornflakes in your new super breakfast mix, then how will they convince the trade buyers, who in turn will convince the public and so on?

Support is more than advertisements. It is sales aids, literature, show-cards, good packaging, and a host of other items all working hard to help move your product.

Will this new line be readily available and easily identifiable among the welter of other products directly or indirectly competing?

Tying in distribution and promotion for a moment: is point-of-sale material essential to clinch our customer? Wrapping a great product (did you remember to test your product on a group resembling the desired market?) in the best packaging is not necessarily enough, unless, by luck, you are a household word. And even good marketers whose wares are household words do not leave themselves open to losing market share to an erstwhile up-and-coming competitor.

In-store presentation means so much today, with more products than ever before fighting for the consumer's spend. It is insufficient to think that volume sales to the end-customer can be assured just by selling the storekeeper thirteen to the dozen with an added bonus for bulk buying. That little old lady reaching for the shelf is your real market. She is the one you must convince.

Use the framework

These essential marketing principles provide a framework for a sensible approach to doing business. In short, you need to learn about your market, plan your product, promote it, and keep improving.

Sadly, one often runs into the negative attitude, 'But what do I have to market?' from people who fail to grasp the principle that, just as products need marketing, so too do services. We will see in 'Marketing the Invisibles' how complex and challenging intangibles can be. They cannot be wrapped, cartoned, canned or bottled. However, intangibles and tangibles alike deserve the same analytical approach.

As an example, consider a building society using the marketing approach. What do people in a particular age group require? Are we structured to introduce a new type of account or savings plan to capture that segment of the market? Shall we be faced with major reorganisation? Will a new division be required? Or are we equipped to develop this policy, train our representatives and management, make slight adjustments to administration – all with minimum disruption?

Will it be profitable? How shall we promote it – to our own people, as well as the public? Do we have sufficient offices and field people to push the scheme along?

How do we present our new scheme? Do we advertise, direct-mail, or simply rely on face-to-face selling across the counter? Will there be further opportunities to keep developing this new policy so that, in the long term, we can plan a range of alternatives in this field?

Our consumer is not a moron. And, if you want to safeguard your existing share of business and increase your share of new business, then you must treat the consumer, the decision-maker if you like, with respect. This is the approach all of us must adopt.

Admittedly, the situation is improving, yet one still gains the impression that far too many decisions are made in high places on the basis of gut feeling.

Today we live in an age of instant communication. Consumers are bombarded with exhortations to buy this and buy that. Electronic advertising has created outstanding opportunities to demonstrate products.

Consumers are becoming sick and tired of being told that 'Y' is better than 'Z', 'A' is bigger than 'B', and 'C' gives more value than 'D' – even if the advertiser merely implies. Our consumer is more sophisticated (and has more to spend). And, being more sophisticated, he or she is that much more selective – proving the point that major decisions must not be made on feeling, opinions and experience alone. In nine out of ten cases, homework should be done to eliminate as much risk as possible.

As inferred above, too many of us pay lip service to marketing. If market-place acceptability is of paramount importance, then it follows that the true marketing approach must be heeded.

Know your market, know your business and, above all, do not let guesswork influence decision-making.

Ample scope for creativity

This move away from seat-of-pants marketing and management is not designed to stifle flair or innovation. Do not think that an emphasis on research and planning leads to paralysis by analysis. There is no reason why it should.

The management tools we are reviewing enable you to differentiate between flair and stupidity. We are advocating an inquisitive business approach to help avoid expensive mistakes.

That inquisitive bias will, when you think about it, encourage a creative, innovative bent anyway. Properly handled, it will help reinforce theories or point out required adjustments; it may well uncover lucrative hidden niches or ghost markets. That is sensible flair as opposed to pure 'guess and hope'.

Innovation must still be governed by a careful judgement: Will this move be for the better? Will it enhance our marketing, systems or people opportunites? Will it improve our bottom line?

By all means be creative. Marketing and planning should be creative, not stifling, crafts. They look forward and outwards. But do not lose sight of reality, and remember that, for every Gillette and Edison, there are legions of failed entrepreneurs and day-dreamers.

Summary

Avoid guesswork and use a marketing framework adapted to suit your business. Learn from the essence of marketing audits – independent, systematic and critical evaluations of a company or industry's entire marketing effort.

The market audit reviews and determines what is being done. It evaluates and recommends what should be done.

As with marketing planning, the audit needs to consider *internal* and *external* standards: what you are doing *inside* to ensure that you are capitalising on trends *outside*. Vital components include:

Internal	External
Plans, planning and controls for markets, products/services	Products/services
	Markets
Organisation, structure and personnel	Customers
	Competitors
Reporting	Trading environment
Use of marketing elements	Trends
Integration of sections	
Training	
Perceptions of organisation by our people	

Once the areas of major importance have been isolated, the appraisal of those areas should start. Appraisals, audits or checks – call them what you will – should not be occasional, crisis-influenced happenings. They should be a regular part of the overall management process.

17

Getting the best out of people

Many marketing plans ago there was a seminar attended by a variety of speakers, most of them learned marketing experts whose utterances we barely recall.

One presentation which has never been forgotten, was delivered by an older gentleman who is probably long gone to the great boardroom in the sky. His message was very simple: much of marketing is connected with people. Within organisations, the way in which we work with our colleagues is very important. He had three golden rules, and they are indelibly branded in the mind: carry a small notebook (to write things down, to avoid forgetting); use the stairs (in other words, go to see people – do not wait for them to come to you); say 'Thank you'.

Ten years later, another astute employer used to frequently remind his management team, 'This company's real assets come up in the lift every morning and leave the building every evening.'

Business is people – living, caring, emotional creatures. The '4 Ps' definition of marketing falls short when it summarises the primary focuses as product, place, price, promotion. There is an essential fifth 'P' – and that is people.

People like to be involved

Treating people well helps a business succeed. It is not a matter of being patronising; rather, one of involving people. Countless marketing audits carried out over the years have repeatedly reinforced that communication theory discussed in an earlier chapter – we are great talkers, but poor listeners. Management does not spend sufficient time listening; management does not say 'Thank you' often enough. The result: the emergence of 'them versus us' cells within organisations. And yet it is so easy to combat these frustrating negatives. Be seen to care; foster open, two-way communication. Are you afraid that the freedom will be abused? It will not be in the majority of instances, because most people do not deliberately spoil privileges.

We have talked with some pretty tough trade union types in the course of organisation audits and have had to extract opinions from hesitant foreigners. It is amazing how open, honest and constructive people are once you've won their confidence.

It is not a case of promising them the earth either; all they seek is a fair hearing. And when someone comes along and says, 'I want to hear what you've got to say: tell me what you think are the business's strengths and weaknesses; I'd like any suggestions you've got as to how we might improve things' – well, be assured, everybody wins. Management receive feedback; staff realise (without any phoney promises being made) that their opinions count.

Stop talking – start listening

Some of the saddest business moments have probably been post-audit when, having presented findings and recommendations, management have said, 'If only we'd called you in years ago, we could have avoided all these people problems.' They are so wrong. They could have avoided the problems simply by listening to people, not talking at them, and, above all, by not assuming that management knew how they felt about working conditions, pay rates, opportunities to progress, relationships between staff and management, etc. These are a few of the things that mean something to people – notice how many are not money oriented.

The personnel function – managing and attending to the human resources – can not be brushed aside. Do not fool yourself that unless you are large enough to warrant a personnel manager or department it does not matter. It does. In the smaller concern, the personnel-related activities need to be attended to by management, even if the 'duties' are shared across a handful of executives.

Stop and think about the investment in staff. It adds up to considerable dollars. Whenever somebody leaves, there is often the hassle of finding a replacement who, in turn, will take a while to settle in and, once he or she has come to grips with the job, may up and leave. Few people settle into jobs for life. From chief executives down, there is a manifest tendency to keep moving. For some, the lure is money; for others – and it could be the majority – it is greater challenges and a better working atmosphere. This once again proves the importance of listening to your people so that you know their goals, aspirations and negative perceptions.

Personnel – far more than hiring and firing

The personnel function is well justified. Securing staff, organising training, maintaining records, considering people for promotion, hearing and dealing with complaints, supervising health and safety – these and the other 'formal' requirements are well documented in a variety of position descriptions. Go a stage further, though, and be aware of the most important requirement: a listening ear coupled with a shoulder to cry on.

A quick word on recruiting: turn to the 'Business' and 'Situations Vacant' sections of the daily press. What do you find? – numerous advertisements encouraging people to apply for jobs. When you seek to recruit, plan your approach very carefully. Put yourself in the place of the reader who might apply for the position.

Write honest advertisements that 'talk' in normal language. Avoid the pap and exaggerated, meaningless pomposity that is becoming the hallmark of many personnel management consultants. Like real-estate advertisements, which also attempt to lure people with hyperbole, the effect can be to put people off.

When you interview people, be prepared. Have your questions organised in advance; make interviewees feel at ease. You will find that the friendly, loose-structured approach wins hands down as opposed to the clinical, form-filling exercise employed by some consultants. There is an art to putting people at ease. Develop it, and handsome dividends will result for all parties.

While on the subject of interviews and prospective employees, here is some more well-proven advice: do not be afraid to tell applicants, 'Sorry, you've missed out.' We have frequently explained to candidates that only one person can get the particular job under consideration. The fast, honest, open approach has always been well received.

Personalised replies are also appreciated. Unfortunately, there are consultants who simply send out a 'You're unsuitable' circularised note. Often these cold kisses of death are administered weeks after the interview (or application – not everyone makes it to the interview). There have even been cases where the job applicant has eventually received the 'Tough luck' circular – and the note has referred to a job for which the person did not even apply!

Check the style, check the candidates

Although some consultants work on a fee basis, you will generally find that personnel consultants operate on a commission or percentage-of-salary-package system. It is expensive, though consultants claim it gets results. When you are working for commissions or percentages rather than fees, there is sometimes a tendency to fall into the trap that many life insurance, real-estate and used-car salespeople fall into: the customer comes second to the commission; dedicated attention loses out to fast bucks. So check the consultants' pedigree; talk with some of their clients; then decide whether their approach and method is best suited to your recruiting needs.

It is very easy for people to describe their occupation as 'consultant'. However, there are professional bodies that grant admission to reputable practitioners. Checking people's reputation and standing before authorising a brief is a sensible safeguard.

One result of personnel consulting has been that many aspiring job applicants are treated like hunks of meat. This, in turn, puts people off applying for jobs advertised by consultants; which means that the employer entrusting recruitment to outside 'experts' eventually wonders why the crop of candidates put forward is so poor – and why their money keeps being spent on advertising the vacancies.

Another cautionary note concerns references. The word processor is a wonderful invention. It means that lawyers can make a fortune by copying the same document and simply changing a key word or name here or there.

The same is true for consultants. Curricula vitae fly back and forth like they are going out of fashion as candidates are peddled from one possible buyer to the other. Flowery words flow to paint a glowing picture – but what about the real, down-to-earth story?

Well, do not take too much notice of written references. There are employers who write glorious testimonials because they are so pleased to see the back of a departing trouble-maker. Insist on referees; talk to people; check facts; use your own initiative to make discreet enquiries. After all, you are investing your money – why cut corners? Why accept things on a hunch and then find you have wasted your money?

Some personnel management consultants may remind you that they provide, say, a 90-day guarantee with the appointee (we did not liken them to used-car salespeople for fun). But just think: how many of us wake up to a person's shortfalls within the first three months of their coming on board? There is settling-in time, a learning curve, and then, hey presto . . . you are well down the track and you discover that you have bought a lemon. So it is back to the consultant, and the cycle starts up again – the commissions to be paid, the CVs to be scanned, the short-listed candidates to be interviewed . . . surely common-sense dictates that we reduce risk at the start, before the final decision to appoint.

There rests our case for personnel planning being integrated with marketing and othe prime-function planning.

Training – it never stops

No discussion on personnel would be complete without a brief reference to training. If the preceding paragraphs have indicated that organisations should give more thought to doing their own recruitment – good. Likewise with training: capitalise on your own resources and your own connections.

There will be times when outside advice is required to help with recruitment and training – just as it can be required to achieve improvements in finance, marketing, production, computerisation or whatever other spheres are deemed to be in need of an independent viewpoint. But do not use outsiders as a constant crutch or at the expense of your own involvement.

Training should not be an occasional event or a method of rallying the troops when the trading chips are down; nor should it be reserved for newcomers. Training, like learning, must extend beyond induction. It must be ongoing.

There is an abundance of outside courses available. Apart from those run by reputable organisations, we are seeing more and more training seminars fronted by a variety of international experts. (We are not inferring that they are disreputable.) Sales experts, time-and-quality-control experts, stress-management experts . . . these experts come in all shapes, colours and sizes. A high proportion of such people have the ability to charge people up – temporarily. When the hype's analysed, however, it is a collection of 'Rah, rah, get out and slay 'em', adrenalin-pumping slogans. Now this can provide short-term advantages, but if you want a more permanent state of improvement that will be of lasting benefit to the company, you should consider developing seminars or workshop programmes relative to your company's and your people's needs.

Training conferences should not be beer-and-pie gatherings where the sales team parade the latest yarns. Work must take precedence over bun fights. Training events should be opportunities to learn, to exchange views, to share problem-solving in group discussions, to encourage interchange between different sections of a company.

Case studies should be developed, relative to your particular trading arena and the type of problems your industry encounters.

Companies all too often wait until there is an exodus, before asking themselves what they are doing wrong on the people front. Yet it is so simple when you think about it. Use outsiders by all means – as advisers, or leaders, or moderators. But, whatever you do, do not overlook the cardinal rule that your people work for you – they do not work for the outside consultants. Perceptive employers and management are an integral part of the training process.

Training – an example of the workshop approach

The moderator – whether an outside consultant or an 'in-house' trainer – assumes the role of course leader. The aim is for this catalyst to achieve cross-flow and sharing of knowledge via group discussions; frank, critical problem-solving sessions (constructive not destructive); and syndicates that handle case studies.

Content and topics should, as far as possible, be developed so that they are pertinent to the company's business – its activities, products/services, etc.

A clearly defined agenda should be used as a guide. It must be flexible; do not be concerned if all main topics are not covered.

Consequently, a series of *modules* provides a useful approach. For example, a course or seminar might cover the mainstream topics – allowing ample time for the group discussions etc. mentioned earlier – and include training videos or films and outside speakers or presentations by executives from company sections other than the one holding the seminar.

The 'workshop' approach relies heavily on involvement. Hence the moderator or leader must be skilled at gaining participation. *Participation* is the keyword.

A workshop accenting *marketing* might be structured as follows (to cover approximately two days):

- *Marketing* – the concept; developments; its application to your company.
- *Interplay* required between all sections to achieve a total marketing approach.
- The place of each major *marketing element* – albeit adapted to suit the company's sphere.
- *Problem-solving* – isolate the company's product/service or operational weaknesses; develop workable solutions.
- *Forward planning* – key aims, objectives, goals.
- *Wrap-up*.

To maintain enthusiasm and interest, film/video screenings and/or 'outside' speakers can be included at appropriate stages. For example, marketing seminars frequently benefit from an address by a customer's purchasing manager. Such a person is able to provide an added dimension by saying, 'This is what I expect from you' – thus providing credence and accurate guidelines to ensure a marketing-oriented approach from your company and your people.

Checklist: how to measure staff perceptions and individual progress

1   **How do your people rate the company in regard to the following:**
    The company's *aims* – how clear are they to staff?
    Trust and openness – are you rated high, medium or low?
    Are *tasks* clearly defined?
    Do people enjoy a sense of *belonging*, feeling that they're truly part of the company?
    Are there *aspects* of the company or its business activities that, in the respondent's opinion, could be *improved?*
    Does the respondent have suggestions on how, if required, *improvements might be achieved?*

2   **Periodic reviews to appraise individual's progress should be measured against factors such as:**
    The *objectives* that govern the respondent's position – are they being achieved?
    Skills and ability
    Effort put into main tasks
    The respondent's *relationships* with other staff and management.
    How much *supervision* the respondent requires.

3   **Depending on the person's seniority, rating may extend to evaluate:**
    Planning – contribution made to helping the company achieve its goals
    Accuracy – forecasting, budget realisations
    Organisation skills – to facilitate achievement of company aims and to direct staff towards such achievement
    Implementation – putting the plans into practice
    Control and discipline – ability regarding follow-up, checking, completion and reporting.

Checklist: points to cover in job interviews

1   **Personal data:**
    Name, address, contact details, age, marital status, family, home ownership, education – achievements, qualifications, current study, interests.

2 **Current employment:**
Company, field (i.e. industry), how long in current role/how long with company, position/s – experience and responsibilities – supervised and unsupervised.
To whom does applicant report?
Who reports to applicant or is under applicant's control/direction?

3 **Application reasons:**
Why is applicant applying for this position?
Why is applicant leaving current position?

4 **Knowledge of your company:**
It is always interesting to see how much 'homework' applicants have carried out after gaining an appointment for an interview. . . .

5 **Previous employment:**
Employers; fields/industries; how long; positions and responsibilities; reasons for leaving.

6 **Main requirements:**
On a 'can do/can not do' basis, or using some scoring technique, determine how the candidate measures up against the *key criteria* governing the position.

7 **General:**
Appearance; communication; personality.
Health.
Attitude towards travelling/away from home (where pertinent).
'Clean' driver's licence?

8 **Salary and benefits:**
Current.
Expected.

9 **References and referees.**

10 **Notice required:**
Arrangements governing termination of current employment.

11 **Wrap-up points:**
Any special attributes applicant believes he or she would bring to role/company? Any aspects requiring clarification before closing interview?

18

Controls, systems, structures – how to make them work

Very few people relish the idea of laying down rules to subordinates, and subordinates usually bristle when asked to commit information to paper. Given ideal circumstances, we should be able to verbally agree on control, responsibility and reporting requirements in organisations. In reality, however, nothing could be further from the truth – human nature being what it is.

Controls and systems need to be developed to ensure that marketing concepts and structures work effectively. Improved communication flow, for example, is only realised with well-developed upwards, downwards and horizontal trails.

Write it down!

Written reports, especially from field personnel, must be meaningful and useful to the company. Representatives invariably moan about their paper-reporting requirements. Do not tolerate excuses – field representatives are especially accountable. Call reports, new business reports, monthly overviews, existing and new business status lists, competitor updates – all these and more should be readily available to management.

Analytical and forecast tables should not merely crunch out numbers. We also need to know how and why those numbers have arisen: unit volume, value, actual versus budget, along with the reasons for plus or minus variance.

Positive meetings – action-oriented

Ensure that meetings are attended by a cross-section of key employees or management. For example, barriers are quickly demolished when production people sit in on sales meetings and vice versa.

This exposure to other sections' activities fosters improvements in communication, understanding of each party's responsibilities and pressures, and more harmonious working relationships. When a positive example is set from the top, you have a much greater chance of earning respect from middle and lower management.

If meetings are to be meaningful, the information and decisions that emerge must be shared, albeit in a modified fashion, with subordinates – our 'top-down' philosophy. Avoid waffle at meetings by preparing agendas in advance.

Make sure that meetings encourage the provision of solutions rather than simply providing a platform where the same old problems and complaints are paraded. To realise this end, disciplined, regular gatherings under firm chairmanship are mandatory. And do not waste time preparing boring, copious minutes. These are generally relegated to waste-paper bins or to files that are never reviewed.

By the time minutes hit the recipients' desks, enthusiasm displayed at the meeting has waned and other pressures are gaining priority. A better approach is to issue 'action-lists' immediately after the meeting and circulate them rapidly – preferably within 24 hours – clearly defining the key points that emerged. For follow-up tasks, include initials and dates indicating who must carry out what, along with the project completion or review deadline.

Job descriptions

A further important control device is the job description or position description. Even a two-man band benefits from this approach: confusion as to who does what is avoided; tasks and functions can be allocated; the key headings provide a basis for reviews of what the company's up to and how it is proceeding.

Now extend the requirement to a larger organisation. People, rightly or wrongly, need direction. Confusion and duplication of tasks are too frequently encountered when we objectively assess the effectiveness of organisational structures.

Job descriptions should explain lines of command and reporting procedures. They should clearly set down responsibilities and authority. Furthermore, they should be open-ended to encourage constructive inputs from people. In this way, suggestions for improvement beyond an appointee's specific sphere can be fostered.

Just as organisations can be too rigid or inflexible, so also can they be too loose or linear in their management style. Both approaches lead to frustration and low morale, which can be so easily avoided. Firmness, fairness, sharing – these are core requirements.

Keep it lean

In structural terms, every business has different requirements. Traditional or textbook recommendations are fine as guides – but do not follow them slavishly. Heed your trading environment, market size, organisation spread, and degree of responsibility vested with individuals. Then adapt the standard formulae to suit your specific environment.

Avoid cumbersome structures that cause decision-making delays or encourage empire-building. Ensure cross-flow and joint efforts by devising an organisation chart that fosters teamwork and joint efforts.

Aim for a system that, above all else, assures sound communication – that is the real guts of success – a system that pushes routine decision-making down to more people, emphasising teamwork and sharing.

People considerations and open communication are often neglected at the expense of too much theory. As with so many management goals, keep the structure simple – a lean, flexible organisation that fosters multi-angle communication.

Share information

When employees are given positive direction and the 'big picture' is shared with them, they usually respond in a keen manner. The importance of the 'employees' is kept in perspective when we envisage a pyramid: (Figure 5).

The apex contains very few people (chiefs); as we descend, the widest section of the triangle represents increased numbers (Indians). It is obvious that effort needs to be geared to displaying sound leadership and the right attitude to that greater proportion.

The 'thinking' approach to organisational structures requires planning. The most common excuse for not fine-tuning or experimenting is 'We don't have enough time.'

Is this really the case, though? Maybe we're copping out; maybe we do have the time but it is not easily identified because we're wasting it – we are inefficient.

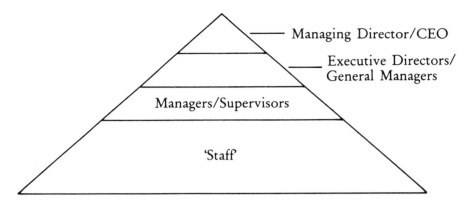

Figure 5

Stopping for interruptions; slipping into a state of crisis management; showing a lack of self-discipline; procrastinating – we are all guilty of such things, some of us more than others.

Save time

The points already outlined in this chapter and in Chapter 8 will help combat such problems. So too will a sound delegation system (more on this topic in the following chapter), priority lists, and customer rankings (to help determine levels of service, as well as the frequency and type of contact).

Keep timesheets so that you know just where your time goes. For years we have encouraged management people to do this, and those who have taken our advice have, after two or three months, achieved greatly improved productivity and better time management.

If we are seeking time-saving, we must check that we are taking advantage of mechanical aids: dictating file notes into hand-held recorders; making full use of the telephone to reduce transport costs and save time; and taking advantage of video and videotext.

Telephones have been around for a long time. Despite this, many representatives will still walk out of their office and drive a company car to a customer's location where a standard repeat purchase will be documented. The same transaction could easily have been completed over the telephone. In fact the representative could probably have delegated the contact to an 'inside' person, thus devoting time to something more expansionary such as a development call.

People may like personal contact, but busy customers appreciate time-saving techniques employed by suppliers – your customers are probably under pressure too.

Overall, we need to check our efficiency, our streamlining, our systems and structures. Computers and other time-reducing hardware certainly help the cause. Nevertheless, it's still necessary to work better and think smarter.

Summary

Active requirements ('doing')

- Selling.
- Sales liaison.
- Servicing existing customers.
- Developing new business/new markets.
- After-sales service.

Passive requirements ('planning')

- Establishing objectives and strategies.
- Monitoring, measuring, and developing techniques.
- Market intelligence and information system.
- Support aids, e.g., advertising, promotion, etc.

Control devices:

- **Job descriptions** should cover responsibilities and procedures, and clarify lines of command and liaison.

- **With call reports, new business reports, monthly reports,** prepare in advance *key headings* covering the information required by the 'receiving' executive and/or company. Set deadlines; ensure they are adhered to. Emphasise that reporting must extend beyond 'historical' information, to cover *forward* proposals and provide *solutions* to problems.

- **Meetings and review sessions** should be based on agendas prepared in advance, including basic information and/or tabulated data – e.g., sales figures for previous period. Disciplined, regular gatherings and firm chairmanship are desirable. Rapidly circulate post-meeting 'action' lists rather than formal minutes.

- **Develop a lean hierarchy and short lines of communication:**

Obviously a large organisation may develop further specialist sections on second-tier levels or as specialist 'advisory units' – quality assurance, technical development, personnel, planning . . . to name a few.

For the *smaller company* such an approach would be neither affordable nor sensible, so you should determine *responsibilities among key executives* to ensure that all essential functions are covered.

Figure 6

19

Letting go – the art of delegation

Delegation goes hand in glove with efficient, effective use of our time. It is the process by which we pass duties, power, or work on to somebody else.

For most of us, it is difficult to let go. We can do the job quicker and better; we know the ropes. We insist on punishing ourselves while we bemoan the fact that our subordinates do not display initiative – they do not seem to care.

As with communication and those other personal skills that have a bearing on marketing and general management well-being, delegation requires constant self-discipline.

Start by analysing your activities. How do you spend your time? Which tasks could be transferred to somebody else?

There is nothing wrong with giving people problems to solve – but do not dump crises in their laps when they are not trained to cope (because nobody has delegated such things to them previously).

When you do delegate, display confidence in the person whom you are entrusting with the project. If worried, do not signal your concern. We all had to learn at some stage or other.

Plan to spread your workload

A reduction of the risk and worry level could result from a little forward planning by the person who is doing the delegating. Establish priorities; do not be backward about asking people if they would like to tackle this task or that task – involvement is then seen to be happening.

Once you have delegated, do not look over peoples' shoulders constantly. Let them get on with the job. By all means check progress, but do so in a constructive manner – one that does not prevent the other person from displaying initiative.

Delegation is not just passing the buck, firing out instructions, or abdicating your responsibilities. It calls for team-work, crystal-clear understanding, and excellent communication.

As with all two-way communication, the messages involve a sender and a receiver. A breakdown between the two invites chaos. That is why the review aspects are important to successful delegation. The 'sender' must be accessible.

When should you delegate? This depends on your business, your employee ranks, and so on. It also depends on facing up to a few home truths: in letting go of a job, are you passing it on to someone who can do the task better, at a lower cost, more productively? Or are you just passing the buck?

When authority is shared downwards, you are enhancing employees' job satisfaction. It also gives superiors more time to get on with planning and thinking ahead, instead of being burdened with repetitive tasks that could provide subordinates with a challenge.

Motivation is a magic something that causes people to act in a particular manner. To improve motivation, the opportunity of facing up to challenges must be given. In a nutshell: most of us want to be told what to do, then we like to be left to get on with the job.

Good company spirit is a contagious disease. It spreads from the top. Showing interest in people means sharing responsibilities around, praising when a job is well done, and correcting in a firm but explanatory manner when something goes awry.

You see, none of us are perfect. We are all capable of making mistakes. If we learn from those mistakes, then some purpose has been served. Wise delegation is an art that should be developed for the good of all concerned.

For the person doing the delegating, many benefits can arise. Not least of these is being respected as a leader of your organisation's people rather than being viewed as the boss.

Summary

Delegation is important because managers need *time* to plan and think ahead. When you delegate, explain

- What is to be carried out.
- When it must be carried out by.
- How the task might be achieved.
- What authority rests with the person to whom you are delegating.

In essence, delegation means this to the 'receiver': 'Tell me what you want me to do, then let me get on with the job.'

Before delegating a task, check that it will be carried out better, cheaper and more productively. After you have delegated a task, do not interfere.

20

Marketing the invisibles

Over the years, we have found it a useful practice to review textbooks from publishers dealing with marketing-related management topics. One addition to our library was entitled *The Marketing of Services*.

Services, or intangibles, are far too frequently neglected as the 'poor relations', the forgotten dimension, of marketing management. Yet look around: you are surrounded by a host of business acitivities that you cannot touch, taste, see or smell. As the book referred to emphasised in an apt quotation from *Business Week*: 'For a fee, there are now companies that will balance your budget, baby-sit your philodendron, wake you up in the morning, drive you to work or find you a new home, job, car, wife, clairvoyant, cat feeder or gypsy violinist.'

An essential aspect of marketing is to identify and satisfy customers' needs. Those needs – visible or otherwise – must be clearly defined and awarded the attention they deserve.

If you consider the services angle for a while, you will quickly realise there is a vast population of organisations that cannot display their wares but still rely heavily on motivating customers or end-users. Banks and building societies, finance houses and insurance companies, travel agents and transport operators, airlines and accountants – an extensive list can be assembled without too much effort.

Services – for too long the poor relation

The marketing of services has, until recently, been downplayed or ignored. Fast-moving consumer goods, home appliances, and high-capital-cost items were invariably under the marketing spotlight.

Purveyors of pet foods scramble to find out what flavour Fido prefers. We gaze in wonder as a procession of television advertisements tell us how we should dress or smell; what we should drive; which beverage slakes the meanest thirst; how not to be caught out when unexpected, famished guests arrive on the doorstep. . . .

However, the winds of change are blowing through the marketing world. Credit cards, debit cards, money-at-all-hours cards; protection for one's home and its contents; luxurious comfort and gourmet food when flying at 40 000 feet; smiling forecourt attendants (at least in the television advertisements screened by oil companies) scrambling to clean your car windscreen . . . at long last marketers are waking up to the fact that they must add sizzle and appeal to services.

Actually, if you are selling a service, you need to pay far more careful attention to marketing detail than your product counterparts. Services demand a particular type of research and development, a distinct approach to selling and promotion. Frequently, the distribution of services is governed by a third party – a shop accepting a credit card to charge goods, for example – which can have a strong influence on your efforts to expand market share.

With services, the invisible benefits must be underscored and translated in a manner that encourages customers to 'buy' and intermediaries to support – you cannot rely on taste, smell, touch or sight.

As society advances, we will witness a growth in the marketing of services. The electronic and computer revolutions have paved the way to a cashless, buy-from-home-in-the-comfort-of-your-armchair-at-the-push-of-a-button generation.

Services and professions cannot count on loyalty

What price loyalty? Zilch. Those days of sticking with the same bank or insurance company for life have vanished. It is in your interest to shop around and find the best deal, the most pleasant people, the widest selection of useful services.

That disappearing loyalty to institutions is also extending to the professions. They are no longer sacred. Dentists accept Visa cards, and doctors are forced to explain to patients what they are prescribing and why.

The deregulation of professions is upon us. We have handled briefs in which advice has been provided to architectural, engineering, valuation and legal companies on how to apply marketing thinking. The professions need to leave their ivory towers and abandon aloofness and jargon.

Professions require a marketing approach

The need to provide a parcel of services has been demonstrated by chartered accountants. Mergers of practices have become common, as has linking up with overseas affiliates. The major accountancy groups are very actively involved in wider consultancy fields, from personnel placement to strategic marketing.

Diversification is probably well founded in many cases, but in some instances one cannot help wondering why they did not stick to balancing books. Hints on selecting advisers appear in Chapter 27 and should be heeded if you're considering an accountancy-based practice for wider management counsel.

Professional groups with deregulation thrust upon them should not panic. Competition will sort out the men from the boys. Initially, there is always a flurry as the big-noters proclaim their brilliance in four-colour magazine advertisements – quite likely a total waste of money. Professionals should not be flashy up front. They need to convey an air of specialisation, security, confidentiality, expertise, independence – and value for money.

Their efforts should be aimed primarily at existing customers, contacts and referral sources – not worrying about the wider market, except perhaps for discreet, occasional, 'card-type' reminder advertisements in selected publications.

Corporate literature – in the form of a guide to what the partnership or practice does, where it operates, and so forth – would probably be their best weapon in the promotion arsenal, aimed at prime customer/referral segments.

Any sensible professional group would probably commence marketing involvement by conducting some basic research – starting with their existing clients and business associates. It is necessary to find out how those customers (clients, if you insist) perceive the practice – and the profession – its services, charges, language, people, and so on.

Yet again, the flexibility of marketing is the guiding beacon. It is the *adaptation* of the principles that counts, the tailoring to suit services, professions and all of those areas where the 'invisible product' jostles for a share of somebody's mind, somebody's hard-earned disposable income.

Presentation – do not frighten your customers

Times change and fashions change – not just dresses, swim-suits, and hairstyles, but colours, décor and architecture. Victoriana may be in vogue for pubs and eating houses but not necessarily for banks.

Today's market, particularly the big-spending youth market, probably appreciates a scene that identifies with their mores – which is something that financial institutions should heed. Anyway, most of us find it rather pleasant to wander into a bright, airy foyer that puts a bit of colour into its image. It need not be cheap and gaudy, but it can easily have an aura that means the difference between feeling you are welcome or not.

If you hide behind a mantle of mediocrity and sameness, contenting yourself with always following instead of making an effort to lead, you cannot possibly hope to have your service prominently positioned in people's minds.

Try to be first with really new benefits. Imitation is still the sincerest form of flattery. Ask someone, 'Who climbed Mount Everest first?' The odds are that they'll say, 'Hillary'. Then ask them, 'Who last climbed Everest?'

Financial institutions leading the way

Travel agents were familiar with the 'retail' nature of their services quite early in the scheme of things, but financial institutions have been slower to learn. Now many are finally grasping marketing thinking. They investigate systems operating in that Mecca of consumer motivation, the United States; they develop a service to suit their local requirements (surveys help them fine-tune); and then they take the wraps off. Big, bold advertisements are used to gain attention and set people talking – advertisements that promise something, that talk about a benefit. Following up their advertisements, some have the good sense to mail to selected customers. The sales package can be completed with a colourful, descriptive brochure outlining the services in detail – how they work, where they apply, and so forth. To cap it off, they include an application form. Smart move – far too much communication money (whether it is spent on media advertising, direct mail, or informative literature) is wasted because it does not invite action.

Consumer reaction to a sincere sales approach stressing service benefits is generally positive. There will always be customers determined to label any new development that is different as a 'gimmick'. However, they are frequently a minority and should not deter any of us from constantly seeking improvements.

Find out what the customer thinks

Where service, professional or quasi-professional organisations are pushing a similar barrow, they really must develop a marketing edge over their competitors. They should take a hard, cold look at the face they are presenting to the customer.

Check your image: Do people think you are making too much money? Are your representatives or advisers well trained? Is training a continuous process so that everyone is right up with latest developments and changes? Are your locations where people most want them? Is some business best carried out in the prospect's home or office? Is your literature up to date and readily understood?

For the protection-related services, the customer views dying or losing everything in a fire as a rather serious matter. It is imperative that the broad workings of insurance schemes can be easily grasped. The essential facts should not be lost in a mire of advertising garbage.

Viewed from any angle, the main rule stays constant: market with flair. The greater the challenge and the more similar the competitors' services, the greater the need for the approach advocated.

To conclude: many readers may say, 'We're already doing these things. So tell us something new.' To me, that's a negative challenge. Whatever you do, you have got to do it that much better in these days of improved communication, discretionary spending power, a mobile society, and so forth.

If you search long and hard enough, you will find a better way of marketing your existing services. It may be a small change. It may call for a radical approach. Ensure that you do your marketing groundwork first; then the investment in time, money and people could pay off with an increased share of business.

Summary

- Service organisations and professions must utilise marketing techniques – adapted to suit their business or activity.

- Honesty and believability are essential.

- 'Talk' to your customers in a language they understand.

- Question or research your existing and potential customers. Find out how they rate your services, charges, benefits and so on.

- Ask existing and potential customers to indicate what they see as forward trends to aid accurate developments.

- Do not overlook calm, believable advertising. If you are in a 'serious' business, flashy advertising could cheapen your image and reduce your credibility.

21

Retail marketing – kill the 'can I help you?' approach

Throughout this book, reference has been made to customers – to people who choose one brand ahead of another, weighing up their purchase options before deciding where to spend their money. Much of that money is channelled through retail outlets, so it would be fair to expect retailers to have grasped and developed the marketing art. Yet very few have.

Lack of interest in the customer is probably the retailer's cardinal sin. All too frequently, the impression gained is that most store or shop salespeople feel they are doing the customer a favour; they hate their jobs; you can take it or leave it as far as they are concerned; the boss is the one making the money – they are not. This is all summed up by that negative approach mentioned in Chapter 8: the bored sales assistant sidles up and says, 'Can I help you?' The general reply is, 'No thanks, I'm just looking.' What price initiative?

The customer is number one

For retailers, the customer is a god. He or she walks into a store and deserves to depart with something, even if it is simply good vibes, a feeling that some interest was displayed. The approach, then, is critical: adopt an adviser role; learn to have information at your fingertips (or know where to obtain it); show genuine concern; do not talk up or down to people; learn about your products and services.

Opportunities abound

There is a world of marketing opportunity waiting to be conquered by enthusiastic retailers. Chances abound to cross-sell, to up-sell, to sell added value. Furniture stores can sell carpets and drapes to complement furniture; after the lounge, there are home appliances for the kitchen and a variety of aids to help people enjoy their extended leisure time.

Travel agents can often start with an airline ticket and move on to ground travel, accommodation, insurance, and a number of other additional revenue-earning opportunities. And the beauty of it all is that you are not hard-selling to your customers – you are merely providing a complete package.

Most of the marketing messages in this book will have a bearing on retailers. A few other points that should not be overlooked are as follows.

Silent language

Merchandising displays and window settings – are they clean, creative, and altered frequently? Are you using them to sell a range or a 'wide' package? Staying with our furniture example: are you projecting an integrated feeling, a total setting?

Direct response and existing customers

People replace most goods on a cyclical basis. Are we utilising captive-customer lists sufficiently and efficiently?

Store demonstrations, in-home trials

Carrying display a stage further: how about low-cost research – asking customers' opinions on preferred products, or organising panel discussions to check trends and tastes.

Stock-turn

Merchandise in the store is not like money in the bank any more. Stocks these days must be kept at a realistic minimum level. Retailers need to strengthen their links with manufacturers and suppliers.

Retail stock earns nothing until you sell it to somebody at a profit – a case for frequent stock-taking to know which lines are moving and which are dead.

Marketing partnerships

Make the most of links and affiliations with suppliers of goods *and* services. Take credit card companies, for example: they rely heavily on the retailer to ensure transaction success. The partnership's a two-way street – credit card companies will generally entertain ideas for special promotions or support, as will wise manufacturers. It is over to the retailer to reveal some flair, a penchant for promotion that says, 'We're better than the others; how about some special deal?'

Benefits from these trading partnerships abound for supplier and retailer alike. The weight and creativity of national promotions can be enjoyed by even a small, local stockist who locks in under the banner of a major supplier. Normally, such an activity would not be affordable for the small operator, but with careful forward planning, the campaign timing can be capitalised on at low cost.

Joint promotions and information sharing

The costs of joint promotions – for example, in the form of media advertising, direct mailings, or merchandising drives – can be shared between principals and stockists. Again, national material produced by principals can often be adapted, giving greater mileage to all concerned; each party's spend achieves double coverage.

Use your links to find out what is happening beyond your trading territory. Regional and national trends, competitor activities, new product plans – national suppliers have a wealth of data at their disposal and they are usually delighted to pass it on to stockists who display interest. Most retailers do not think to ask for such information.

In addition to informative pamphlets, brochures and other sales aids, check the availability of video material and audio-visual devices. These can be used for staff training to increase product knowledge or, in some cases, for in-store screening to attract customers' interest or create store traffic.

Co-operative activities carry more financial muscle and more credibility. They enable the smaller dealer to foot it with larger counterparts. Size does not preclude initiative and imagination; frequently it is the squeaky door that gets the oil – which simply means that a retailer should get alongside suppliers and capitalise on the relationship before competitors do.

Indirect competition

Retail trade is not restricted to stores selling goods. For instance, banks and travel agents are essentially in the retail business.

Let us say somebody owns a furniture or appliance store. During a weekend, you have browsed at their window display or been alerted by their catalogue, which arrived in your letter-box. Come Monday, you decide to wander along and take a look at what they are offering.

On the way, you pass banks and other savings institutions (encouraging you to put your money to work); or your eyes are drawn to a travel agent's display (escape, pleasure, adventure); or you walk by other furniture or appliance traders – and you start comparing.

You see, it is not only the active effort you make, but also the way in which passive elements – advertising, promotional aids, displays, and so on – work hard for you that counts.

Design is becoming an increasingly major influence in retailing, and particularly with the trend to segmentation of outlets by demographic groups and lifestyles. Retailers ignore this new dynamic market environment at their peril.

Retailers need to plan their marketing approach in the same disciplined fashion as any other sector.

Now reread the chapters on marketing, general management, and planning if you have not already figured out how the guidelines influence retailers. . . .

22
Export – salvation or commercial suicide?

The shrinking of the global trading arena, with its rapid transport and communication devices, has led to the catch-cry for many becoming 'The world's our market!'

Exporting, or offshore trading as some prefer to call it, suddenly emerges as the ideal way to solve trading ills. Just grab a ticket, pack a bag with samples, and hey presto – 'We're off to conquer lucrative new markets abroad.'

In the best greener grass next-door tradition, companies that were finding the going tough in the home markets, with which they were at least familiar, looked enviously at export markets as their new salvation. Unfortunately, such overseas markets have all the complexities of home business and a few more as well.

Avoid a hit-and-miss approach

As the export catch-cry spread, samples were assembled and numerous manufacturers jumped on the export bandwagon. They charged off, expecting to return with full order books. Unfortunately, many of these would-be international merchants were little more than ill-prepared order-takers wandering into Noddy Land.

Is this a harsh judgement? Not so. There was one group of furniture manufacturers who thought that big bucks were to be made at a home-furnishing fair in Los Angeles. Once on board the aircraft, *en route* to the fair, their main objective was to see how much free airline booze could be consumed. 'Who needs to prepare for the sales mission anyway? We will worry about the details when we get there . . .'

The first drawback was that our ace exporters' timing coincided with a public holiday period. There were not too many potential buyers around . . . Result: the participating exhibitors left their furniture behind on consignment.

Export is not the answer for the sloppy, self-confessed entrepreneur who thinks overseas trading is an excuse for having a ball away from home. There are not, these days, too many who fit that description. But, every now and then, some wild-eyed trading Messiah says, 'Let's export' – in an endeavour to solve a host of domestic market problems.

Export may well be part of the economic-survival prescription for small 'island' nations or countries with excess capacity and production overflows. At the same time, however, the demand for professional, planned effort cannot be overstated. Export requires total commitment from the top down in any organisation.

Export is not glamorous

Although, for many, export appears attractive, it is not an easy task. Only poets, visionaries and idiots think that exporting is simple or glamorous.

Export is worthwhile. Acknowledging that small countries have small home markets; and acknowledging that many manufacturers have excess capacity; and acknowledging that manufacturers are often faced with inordinately high set-up costs for sophisticated machinery . . . it soon becomes apparent that a larger demand 'pool' needs to be sought in order to justify investment and establish economies of scale.

Local markets should not be neglected – government whims abroad can, overnight, eliminate an export market. Keep reminding yourself that export is something to widen your opportunities, but do not get too restricted, too reliant on an overseas market that could be subject to fluctuations or dumping.

Our global-market trading centres are now merely hours, not months away. The shrinking of the world means that solid export opportunities can be uncovered by wise, careful traders.

Concentrate on profitable niches

Forward planning, thorough investigation (including as much homework as possible from your base before setting out), and the careful isolation of markets into workable segments are just three 'start-up' rules.

Some markets abroad have a constant demand for products that cannot be fully satisfied by local sources. Segment them to identify those regions or areas best suited to your enterprise. Markets that are small by international standards may be quite large by your standards – more than one exporter has been caught on the hop when the prospective customer has placed a 'minimum order' – an order of a magnitude impossible to fill using current equipment and facilities. Concentration may be better directed at markets that, by offshore standards, are deemed small yet are ideally suited to your production capacity.

Patience and perseverance must not be overlooked. Repeat calling to win confidence, to learn about the market, to improve your understanding of the people with whom you are dealing. Customs, idiosyncrasies, regulations, languages, life-style – it is a complex business. Arabs do things differently to Chinese; Japanese have a different physical build from Americans.

Watch the regulations and methods

Then there are varying distribution systems. Study these too. Some countries have an emphasis on purchasing associations; others on viewing wares at trade fairs or exhibitions. Trading houses that deal in a variety of products may be your only entrée into selected markets.

Financial and production aspects interweave: tax deductions, incentives, grants, payment methods, exchange risks, the effect on local stockholding and distribution (you cannot jeopardise the franchise won at home).

As we have already mentioned, a government can alter the picture in a flash. Revolutions in volatile dictatorships aside, the political scene in your own backyard can heavily influence export. Devaluation, currency rises – there are many possibilities.

As with planning guidelines, volumes have been written on what to do/how to do it with reference to export marketing. Some of the main pointers are as follows.

Joint efforts

Do not overlook shared resources. We are not necessarily competing against our fellow manufacturers when we venture abroad; we are competing against the rest of the world. Consider joint funding of investigations, shared missions on a roster basis, joint promotional catalogues, and so forth.

Look to the end-market

Indirect exports are frequently neglected – track other exporters' products to discover what part your products or services can play in helping these customers achieve foreign sales.

Do not count on government promises

Do not take too much notice of government utterances at home. Successive ministers from different parties will talk a great deal about what they are going to do. 'Talk' is the operative word. When it comes to assembling the best talent to spearhead task groups or new ventures, it still seems to be 'jobs for mates', irrespective of the colour of the party in power.

Use free advice

Avail yourself of all the free advice that is around. There are institutes, associations, banks, government trade centres, and others brimful with information – much of it free for the asking. Certainly, in some instances, 'user pays' must apply. Nevertheless, you will find the services economical and valuable.

Check constantly

Check, check, check and double-check. Do not risk dissipating time and money on vague ideas; focus only on the best concepts.

Put yourself in the place of the overseas customers. Consider how farmers, producer boards, and our government's 'talking heads' beat their breasts because of things like meat and butter mountains. Those mountains are simply monuments to farm-gate mentality – refusing to accept that the whole world does not love lamb, that some nations want meat cuts and not carcasses.

Markets could be closer than you think

Look into freight content and distance. It may pay you to leave faraway places to travel agency brochures. Do your research at home and identify potential opportunities. As already mentioned in Chapter 3, there is a great deal of valuable information available on overseas markets, but you have to look it out.

In Europe, countries like the UK, which had traditional international trading links with the Commonwealth countries, the USA and the Far East; and also France, West Germany and Italy are rethinking their priorities and developing strategies to exploit the Single European Market which will exist by 1992.

For mainland America, scrutinise a world map. Consider the distance between the east and west coasts. It is pretty obvious where to start is it not? And for America, do not read 'states' – one small part of one single state could ultimately become more market than you are capable of handling.

Export development can provide opportunity. Success requires tenacity, a continuing ability – physically and mentally – to withstand knockbacks, and a dedicated approach to systematic marketing planning.

There are no ifs or buts with export marketing. It is neither a quick way to foreign exchange riches nor a panacea for a country's economic woes.

Unfortunately, there are still some misinformed people who believe that export trading is a perk involving exotic activities at equally exotic destinations – or a wonderful tax fiddle, or something you dabble in when things are quiet on the home selling front. Nothing could be further from the truth.

Summary

- Establish accurate objectives.

- Check market potential.

- Do your desk work before heading into the field.

- Research the market – if it is 'Go':

- Check regulations and tax situations.

- Establish pricing policies – heed additional costs, packaging and freighting methods.

- Determine market niches – do not adopt a 'worldwide' approach.

- Establish financing and payment procedures.

- Determine your current organisation's suitability in terms of staff and systems to handle export.

- Check your production capacity. Are any product adaptations required?

- Check promotion methods and aids.

- Check language and design requirements (some colours and symbols have different meanings in different countries).

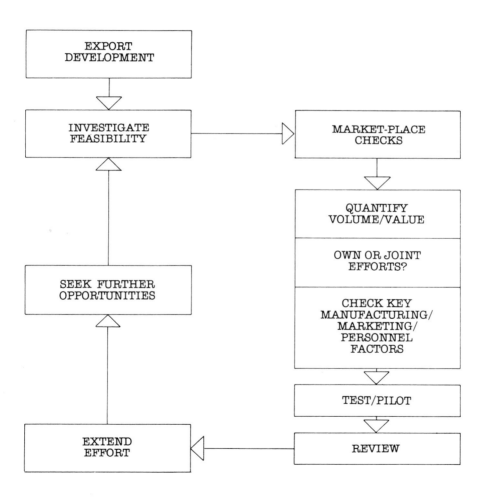

Figure 7

23

Marketing in the national context

Logic suggests that there should be a correlation between what might be termed the marketing dynamism of a country and its economic prosperity. Certainly, over the centuries nations have fought wars to gain control of raw material or basic commodities in undeveloped parts of the world and have then sold finished products back to the countries within their control. Many of the great empires were built for this reason and were essentially captive markets.

Similarly, control of trading routes served the same purpose, and both could be considered to be early versions of a controlled marketing philosophy.

However, as traditional empires waned and industrialisation spread, with international competition in its wake, national philosophies changed and the increased involvement of governments in basic industries and services made it essential that marketing thinking was part of national policy making.

Governments also became aware of how much taxation, exchange rates, interest levels, industrial regulations, environmental controls, health care, pensions, defence spending, investment and international agreements, could impact on company trading performance, and on matters of national concern like industrial output, share of world trade and unemployment.

If a country's unemployment level is examined against its ranking on the international marketing dynamism league, there is a clear correlation, as there also is on industrial performance.

The approach nations take to marketing themselves varies widely and the country which has done the most effective marketing job over the last four decades has been Japan. It carried out a thorough analysis of likely industrial, technological and social changes in world economies, and developed strategies that gave it international leadership and virtual domination of many new, high tech, growth markets. 'Made in Japan' took on a whole new meaning as they developed and sold products that were specifically designed to meet the carefully researched needs of customers around the world, and they used new technology to provide quality and performance standards previously unknown in mass manufacturing. Now, having virtually taken over many world markets for consumer goods, they are about to do the same in industrial markets.

West Germany, Scandinavian countries and the USA have set the marketing pace in other spheres, and over the next decade the revitalised UK, Spain and Korea are likely to make the running, but in quite different ways and from quite different backgrounds and traditions.

Just as the chief executive and the board have to establish the right market orientation and strategies in a company, so also must the leader and government of a country. Isolationism and protectionism are no longer meaningful philosophies even for the super powers, and the reality of this is exemplified as the EEC countries move to the complete removal of trade barriers by 1992.

Marketing nations

In addition to the need for marketing a nation's expertise and products in manufacturing and services to the international community, there is the other side of the coin – attracting investment and tourism into the country. Governments have a prime role to play in creating the environment, infrastructure, facilities, skills and financial incentives appropriate to the customers they are trying to attract.

A country has to assess its strengths and weaknesses, its competition, the key aspects of markets it is targetting, what its competitive edge is, and how it should be packaged and presented to maximum effect.

Countries are essentially very complex businesses and marketing philosophy and disciplines are just as essential.

Internal marketing

Governments, and opposition parties, also need to pay heed to marketing themselves and their policies to their home audiences.

Over the years politicians have become inceasingly aware and skilful in their use of promotional and advertising techniques, but unfortunately they have made the same mistake that many companies made in thinking that the very visible tip of the marketing iceberg was all that mattered.

Unless the market and customer research has been carefully done, and the right product imaginatively designed and developed, it is unlikely to be bought by the voters, no matter how slickly it is presented.

And when governments want to introduce new policies and programmes, or effect basic attitude or cultural change in a country, as the UK, Spain and now the USSR are doing, marketing thinking and disciplines are necessary to convince the customer that the product is the one he or she should buy.

Summary

- Marketing principles are as relevant to the running of a country as they are to managing a corporate business.

- Leaders, governments and politicians generally should appreciate marketing thinking and disciplines.

- They need to listen to their customers, understand and anticipate their requirements and communicate their product message effectively.

- They also need to be fully aware of the changing national and international environment, and adapt to it.

24

Quality assurance – its impact on marketing

Having taken a leaf out of the Japanese marketing book in the previous chapter, it is appropriate to devote a brief section to discussing the link between marketing and quality.

Marketers determine, by examining the market place, whether a real (as opposed to imagined) need exists for a product or service. Manufacturing and production departments advise whether the product is viable to run; the financial people calculate profitability and other value/volume dimensions.

Acknowledging that marketing is a total management philosophy caught up in that synergy of prime business functions dealt with earlier, it is clearly essential to produce high-quality goods and services – that is, if you covet repeat business and ongoing customer satisfaction. That is where quality assurance, quality control and specifications provide governing bench-marks for success.

Avoid failure, ensure repeat business

The high cost of failure is in itself a compelling argument for supreme quality standards. Remember an earlier comment on product failure: something like 95 per cent of new products fail somewhere between the drawing board and the market place.

Do people buy on quality or price? To reinforce earlier arguments, it is worth relating how a New Zealand company became involved in marketing a high-technology, multi-layer packaging film in the United Kingdom. This company succeeded in capturing the market from European suppliers – although the New Zealand prices were higher – because of superior product performance and outstanding quality features.

Value for money/satisfaction

Low-cost or impulse purchases aside, the crucial factor is value for money every time. Quality, reliability, problem-solving, service – these are the buyer priorities repeatedly uncovered by our ongoing research. Sure, price is there, but it is not at the top of the list as a prime decision-making factor.

What about export implications? Many countries need to export or perish. It is global warfare out there. The world wants reliability, service and the highest possible quality standards. Reputation in terms of a serious export approach must be established.

Reducing quality means wasting your investment in research, promotion, selling and distribution. Overseas, the problem is heightened because of the distance from home, as well as different cultures, languages, life-styles and regulations. In the United States, home-grown car, shoe, textile and steel industries – to name but a few sectors – are being bled white in the face of imports from Japan, Taiwan, Korea, China and Hong Kong. But is it simply lower prices and overseas competitors' lower wage rates that have caused the revolution? Could quality be caught up in there too?

Protect yourself by instituting a feel for quality and 'getting it right first time' throughout your organisation. As with planning, *involve* people – and not just management either. Get right down to those employees on the factory floor. That is the engine-room where the quality boilers are stoked – or allowed to burn out.

Summary

- Failure costs are high.

- Maintain high standards.

- People, generally, do not purchase solely on price.

- Poor quality or a decline in standards can cause irreparable commercial damage – and destroy your investment in research, promotion, selling or distribution.

- Everybody within an organisation is caught up in quality – quality of products/services; quality of work; quality of systems.

- Involve people in quality circles and quality reviews. Encourage them to suggest improvements.

25

Trading results can aid marketing

Once upon a time, in those halcyon days before stock exchanges, share indices, blue-chip investments, and the like, we had a barter system. It was pretty simple too. If we had a pig – preferably fat and meaty – the odds were that we would set up an exchange deal and our pig would end up in your cave. Meanwhile, we would have gained some grain, a wife or two, or whatever we agreed on as fair terms.

With the advent of money, the system became a little more complicated. Today, the requirements are more demanding than ever before. Buyers want an assurance that the wares they are purchasing or acquiring are offering them best value for money.

Accepting that a function of marketing is to present the wares – or, in the case of the exercise we are going to consider, the up-to-date financial goings-on of a company – there has to be some way in which our potential investors/customers can see for themselves the quality of the 'merchandise'.

If we acknowledge that the 'money product' is an intangible type of commodity, then very special care must be taken with its presentation. In sum, 'A' wants to determine that he is getting as good a buy as possible from 'B'. When all is said and done, the whole business of assets, liabilities, backing per share, tax-paid profit, and so on can be rather difficult to follow. It is not easy to be sure of what you are buying. So one of the general reactions is to learn as much as possible about the particular company's financial affairs – and most people want to find out in the easiest manner possible.

You cannot just wander into a large public company and ask them to let you count the money in the cash register. Yet that is what we really need to do. The customer wants to take stock and see how the performance of a potential investment stacks up in financial terms.

Hence the importance of the annual financial report or trading results summary – an importance that is often sadly overlooked by companies preparing such documents for circulation and outside scrutiny.

Annual reports must extend beyond financial data

Some readers would argue that an annual report's main role is to present financial data. This is not denied. However, the same document can – and should – serve a variety of other support functions as well.

Perhaps one of the problems that has contributed to some lack of acceptance of the annual report's ancillary role has been the marked gap in understanding between marketing people and accountants. Granted, this is not so in every case, but the generalisation rings true in most situations. Often, marketing people have only themselves to blame. They have not always marketed their own craft sufficiently. If, as you read this, you feel you are in that position, pause a moment and ask yourself what you have done to explain the benefits of a sound marketing approach to your accountant, company secretary or financial director.

Dyed-in-the-wool accountants will always feel that the marketing manager is wanting to spend far too much money on blue-sky thinking. But, just as marketers can be trained to think in terms of profitability being an integral part of any marketing project, so too can an accountant be taught to appreciate that the investment in marketing-support items can be justified if one cares to look beyond the figures in isolation.

Get to grips with what is behind the figures

Many marketing people have been guilty of not making sufficient effort to grasp some of the basics of financial management. Yet they expect others to agree with the logic of often untried and unproved marketing strategies. It does not matter if you do not understand how the figures add up, why they are placed where they are. It is essential, however, to appreciate the deeper meanings of the financial side, so that you, in turn, can translate this raw data into communication that other lay people can readily assimilate.

Having said that, and perhaps unearthed one of the main reasons why accountants are too often left to their own devices, let us return to the case in point and review some of the guidelines that help determine whether or not an annual report is in fact fully playing its part as a marketing aid in terms of communication (especially to the non-financial sectors) and presentation.

Understandable language

Rule number one is to remember that an annual report need not be a jumble of figures, meaningful solely to the initiated or readers with a bent for figures. It is very important that the overall 'picture' be composed in the best possible manner.

Just as the illustration for an advertisement or piece of promotional literature warrants careful creative planning, so too does the treatment of our financial 'picture'. Beyond the balance sheet, the same applies to all sets of figures presented in an annual report. Of equal importance are the narrative passages in an annual report – that is, the 'word' sections.

It is a strange thing, but when we talk about the need for advertisements to communicate in meaningful language to selected audiences, we tend to forget that the same applies to other items – items that may not appear in newspapers or magazines or on radio or television. Yet surely anything that carries a company's name or message is passing information to someone about that company – including its annual report. Take just as much care with the language it speaks. After all, money is a very serious matter.

Explain your case

Imagine a company that has the misfortune to suffer a year of decline. Just because the balance sheet and other financial components are not reflecting the progress of a year or so ago, does one write the company off? Now this is where the annual report can work just as hard as any other marketing tool employed by a progressive company.

The figures may appear to indicate, at first glance, that things are a bit sick. Nevertheless, the company could be in pretty good shape. Why did events turn out the way they did? Why were forecasts proved wrong? What contributed to the downturn? Were there factors beyond management's control that caused a decline? What is predicted for the next fiscal year? Was our hypothetical company unduly affected by a change in seasonal demand for products? Was there less money in circulation, meaning that consumers could not maintain purchases at previous levels? Was there an unavoidable lack of raw materials because of overseas supply problems? Were there extraordinary work stoppages during the previous year?

That is only a starter, but it lays out the types of questions that, if asked of your company, might account for what at first glance appeared to be an unhealthy trend. So the annual report can be used to report, as its name suggests, on what happened. Shareholders will thus be reassured that their investment is safe. Potential investors will be aware of factors that contributed to the situation. More importantly, the company can declare what steps it is taking, or has taken, to rectify matters.

Reveal your plans

Marketing textbooks are full of case studies examining companies forced to make major adjustments to their product ranges in order to stay up front as market leaders. Consider the capital expenditure, the massive investments, that had to be made in order to advance. History is littered with examples of both sudden and gradual changes that have made certain products either redundant or, at best, less popular.

Transistors pushed valves aside; women chose nylon ahead of silk; men became tired of cutting themselves with razor blades and took to electric razors (for a while); tear-tab cans have many fans these days; tourists decided that pure jet was the way to fly; wool had battles with a host of synthetics.

The very people most affected by the switches in consumer demand are often the self-same people who are heading the development of alternatives to satisfy the new consumer requests. Just think how much money might be involved and the way in which those sums might twist financial performance for a period. And yet the reasons – the facts – can be communicated in a believable and reassuring fashion.

Consider how a thoroughly prepared annual report can work hard for a company through sound explanations for certain trading events. Naturally, the same argument applies to good news. The annual report can very effectively present this in a tidy manner and help a company greatly with its overall promotion of image – especially as reports tend to lie around for a year or more. Very often they are referred to well after publication for facts about a company. All the more important, then, to ensure that they carry the right message, along with a summary of performance for the past five, ten or more years. In short, the annual report can succinctly give the reader an overview on current and past trading and, in some instances, a peep at future directions and intentions.

We tend to think too much about the marketing applications for the 'real' benefits of companies. As a consequence, opportunities are often bypassed. That is why, in the case of services and competitive edges outside of the 'product' area, extra attention must be paid to identifying and vigorously promoting your benefits.

Market the financial aspects

A British author, Edwin Ornstien, contends in his book *The Marketing of Money* that the classic principles of product marketing apply to money offers. The same can be said for the presentation of financial data. Ornstien argues for a reorientation of outlook and methods in the area we are discussing. There are problems, but these problems can be overcome by using techniques not unlike those employed when marketing merchandise.

With a 'real', as opposed to intangible, product or service, the benefits can usually be observed – touched, tasted, heard, used and so on. When you are communicating the financial side of your business, these benefits are not as readily visible. More so in the case of an enterprise with money as its product. Insurance companies, banks, building societies and the like can make tremendous use of a prestigious annual report as an excellent marketing aid.

Checklist: what to include in your annual report

If the attention paid to figures and financial data mirrors that paid to tangibles, the following guidelines could apply:

1 **Performance:**
   How did we do last year (not only in isolation, but also in comparison to other years)? What were the major contributing factors, for our business and perhaps for all others in our industry?
   Use simple, readily absorbed graphs, charts and so on to reveal in summary form what the detailed financial report is saying.

2 **Pedigree:**
   Who and what is the company? Do not presume that everyone who refers to your annual report knows all about you. Tell readers what you do, how you've grown, and so on. Perhaps there have been affiliations in the past year that have strengthened the company.
   Have your development people come forward with something new that will motivate investors to show increased interest in your company?

3 **Our market/s:**
   Whom do we aim to motivate with our annual report? Just as products have identifiable markets, so too do annual reports. There may be a number of markets, each with differing requirements. It may be necessary to widen coverage for a variety of sectors: stockbrokers and chartered account-

ants who will be acting as referral sources, advising clients on investment, and thus seeking certain professional information; public investors who prefer to sift through information and make their own decisions; clients and prospects who will be able to gauge the company's standing and decide whether or not they wish to become associated with it.

The presentation of accounts and financial information should meet any ethical or legislative requirements, while at the same time conveying the messages in a manner easily absorbed by the less initiated. Assume that, in many cases, the reader will not know an unappropriated profit from an excess cost over book value; ensure that the layman will understand what the figures are talking about. Should the non-accountant type want more detailed information, in a technical sense, an expert can be consulted. Hence the need for the annual report to appeal to a variety of markets.

4   **Format:**
The overall appearance should be one of 'pick me up and read me' – a clean, uncluttered presentation of facts and figures, taking pains to avoid a dull, uninteresting document. Do not fall into the trap of preparing a first-class cover, only to have the interior of the annual

report let the project down. Design and produce the item as a whole. The best presentations make good use of illustrative techniques to give an easily understood picture of what was going on in such-and-such a company.

5   **'We cannot afford that sort of money':**
That lame excuse will not wash. You do not need a technicolor production on paper, but an annual report can rise above the mundane without costing a fortune.

Use coloured paper for selected pages; use a typeface that is a bit different from bread-and-butter Times Roman, which appears in most newspapers.

Instead of announcing 'Annual Report, 1986, XYZ Company Limited' and leaving it at that, make your cover work hard for you. Commission a striking design. And do not think that to achieve this you have to be a major trader, located in a main centre, or that you must retain the services of a big advertising agency. There are plenty of dependable commercial artists and printers around who will bend over backwards to help companies produce a stylish annual report.

6   **Expect further gains:**
Among other things, a well-thought-out approach to pre-

paring and presenting an annual report could result in an improved image, not only among your publics, but also among your own staff.

Companies too often overlook their own people as mobile public-relations officers for their wares or services. The annual report can be used to keep your people up with play and summarise the year's activity. Staff may often be in the position of referring to the report more frequently than anyone else, especially if they use it as a ready source of company information to aid selling, preparing submissions, etc. The same report can provide a summary guide for prospective employees, assisting your recruitment activities and helping induct newcomers.

A better understanding of your company's business can lead to a growth in confidence. This, in turn, can result in buying decisions made in your favour thanks to the fact that information on your company was better set out and more positive.

Interest shown by financial writers and broadcasters may increase. The media can communicate on a far wider basis than your report. If you are blessed with favourable headlines and complimented on the presentation of your trading results, you are earning valuable bonus points.

7 **Direct-marketing applications:**
An annual report can be an additional item in the sales force arsenal: a mailing document for key prospects (be they existing or potential customers), a door-opener or conversation-starter for that hard-to-convince financial director who does not have all day to listen to presentations. It can be circulated among tomorrow's customers or influencers, including commerce and accountancy students, who frequently consider and evaluate the financial reporting of companies as part of their study – and may be potential future employees.

Over the years, you will find that your approach to the task varies. If you take the time to establish a good pattern early in the piece, you will automatically encourage further improvement. By reviewing past efforts, you will continue to set high standards.

With such an attitude, a company will develop a philosophy that says, 'We want to look best.' If you do that, the odds are that you will steal a march on your competitors – or at worst stay up with the leaders. Either way, you will be much better positioned than an also-ran.

Make sure that your annual report is going to work hard for you as a marketing aid. Then get as much mileage as possible out of the publication – by marketing it at every opportunity.

26
You cannot stand still

Staying alive in a business sense means accepting that change is inevitable and constant. The speed of change can certainly vary, but today's inclination is towards the fast lane. Business people owe it to themselves and those for whom they are responsible to be right up to date with the commercial play.

It is no use relying on your accountant to tell you how you stand at the end of the financial year. You often need to know cash and liquidity situations daily.

There is little point in having surplus funds sitting in non-interest-bearing current accounts overnight or during the weekend – your money needs to be working for you.

Today's new breed of hungry, lean management graduates have had more history to learn from than their older counterparts. The latter can frequently contribute more experience. So it follows that capitalising on a combination of learning and experience is important.

Keep learning

The learning curve does not stop. Accept change – fast change at that – and be prepared to extend your knowledge. This does not mean becoming a walking encyclopaedia on every facet of business. Rather, it involves staying up with relevant issues – not necessarily absorbing every detail, but at least having a basic familiarity with them and, most importantly, knowing who to call on for assistance and when. The market place and the trading environment do not stand still; neither does the astute manager.

Learning, ongoing learning, does not mean returning to the classroom. When running training seminars, one of our favourite ploys would be to ask attendees to raise a hand if they had read a book on marketing or management matters within the last couple of months. The show of hands was frequently disappointingly small in number. Yet public and institute libraries are crammed with books that are vital background reading if you want to stay abreast of events and developments. Establishing your own reference library and press- or magazine-cuttings files can be a wise move. Quite apart from books, business sections of the daily press, local and overseas business magazines, along with trade newsletters and bulletins, deserve to be scanned. Periodic involvement in a useful seminar or refresher course is also recommended.

Someone once said: 'Brains are the cheapest thing to buy.' The moral of that phrase could be: do not hold back on seeking expert advice. If the problem requires consulting outside people, do not try penny-pinching 'self-help' measures.

An abundance of both government and independent advisory services exist. Knowing where to go for help is the smart trick.

Check your presentation ability

At the risk of misquoting, here is the sense of an ancient Chinese proverb: 'You can't tell whether a man is a fool until he opens his mouth and speaks.' The message is crystal-clear: if you find it difficult to speak in public or to motivate your people or to handle media encounters, then it is time to change.

The instant, electronic era is a demanding master. Very few people are comfortable under the glare of television lights; live interviews can be soul-destroying – who knows what the interviewer is going to ask next? An in-house video is to be produced – terror sets in. How will I look? How will I sound? What will staff think of me?

Salvation is at hand. Although specialist courses do exist to help tongue-tied, knee-knocking executives, our own advice is to become involved in service groups or an organisation such as Toastmasters. You will soon learn to think before you speak, along with many other tricks of the wise communicator's trade.

Accepting this era of rapid change and applying its implications to our management and self-improvement techniques is a must. We need to be well read, articulate, and in command of a broad range of issues.

Marketing, in fact total management, finds itself pressured by growing social, environmental and consumer forces. Staying up to date is a prerequisite for personal and corporate leadership.

Summary

- Change is constantly taking place.

- Critical faculties must be honed if we are to sort the wheat from the chaff.

- Do not be afraid to say, 'I don't know. I'll find out.' Know when and where to seek advice.

- Read and retain information from newspapers, trade or technical journals and business magazines.

- Attend courses or seminars to widen your knowledge and increase your skills.

- Ensure that your people are exposed to the preceding points and institute ongoing learning opportunities for them.

27

How to use outside advisers

In order to get on well with bank managers, it pays to tell them everything you are up to – how your business is progressing. Keep them posted on your plans.

You should also take outside advisers into your confidence; keep them in the picture. Professional advice can be expensive or cheap, not only in terms of price, but also in terms of the quality of the counsel you receive. At all costs, then, avoid the 'garbage in, garbage out' risk.

Jokes aside about consultants being people who borrow your watch when you ask them the time, bear in mind that any relationship between an organisation and outside advisers depends on mutual trust, personal chemistry, and a host of other two-way criteria.

Independence and objectivity are strengths that the person not enmeshed in the day-to-day affairs of a company may well introduce. The same person must display an ability to quickly develop an understanding of your business.

Empathy is necessary. An organisation that is 'buying' a consultant, advertising agency, market research firm, chartered accountant, legal specialist or any other form of 'outsider' must ask itself how well it can work with the people who will be involved. Do those outside people understand precisely what is required?

Sound briefings

The standards of briefing and information shared will help determine the quality of a project. There is an art to preparing briefs. The honest, open revelation of facts and figures is a priority; crisply written outlines will help the consultant (and save you money). Rambling to a consultant for two hours does not constitute a good briefing. As with planning, 'write it down' is the rule.

Check what you are buying

Be wary of those who tout for business with lavish promises of finding you better people, giving your marketing a shot in the arm, creating brilliant advertising for your product, or saving you a fortune in overheads. Flash up front is usually a cover for fast-buck operators who, as likely as not, have a short stay in independent consulting before moving on to some other occupation. Unfortunately, there is no law against calling oneself a 'consultant'.

Organisations, registers and institutes do exist. However, that 'people chemistry' must not be downplayed. When shopping around for consultants, agencies, accountants, lawyers or any outside advisers/ helpers, do not be overwhelmed by their client lists – ask them what they have achieved for their clients. Then check your business contacts for verification of pedigree.

Don't just flick through the Yellow Pages. Bodies such as the Institute of Marketing and the Institute of Management Consultants have registers and publish handbooks of marketing and management consultants, with details of specialisations, codes of practice, fees etc.

Then there is a host of business-related groups, including management institutes, chambers of commerce, and state-funded associations that can provide guidance. And we should not overlook business studies and commerce faculties at universities. The last-mentioned can often provide undergraduate or postgraduate assistance.

Be wary of consultancies, agencies or professional practices (with deregulation, some chartered accountancy and legal firms seem to think that trendy advertising creates trust) who use large advertisements to tell the public at large how wonderful they are.

It is better, as a 'buyer', to seek recommendations from business associates or other 'neutral' sources. Many of the best assignments and longest standing consultant/client relationships have grown from approaches resulting from enquiries raised with an existing client or institute.

Give a free rein for better results . . .

Consultants usually benefit from being given a free rein. That is where the two-way trust comes in. As with employer/employee relations, frank and open communication between the parties is of primary importance. The most satisfying gain from consulting is knowing that some clients have described it as an extension or part of their business. That provides the urge to contribute over and above the norm.

. . . But do not lose control

Watch out for advisers who give lots of orders, make lots of noise, but rarely provide meaty written reports, sets of guidelines, or time frames. Consultants should display a willingness to put in the same amount of effort and discipline as they expect from your people. That way, they earn the respect of your staff and become viewed as colleagues rather than threats.

You are the client; the adviser is the supplier. The adviser is accountable to you. You do not owe the adviser a living. Achieving the right blend between your organisation's resources and the outside contribution means that you'll be able to reflect on your *investment* in outside advice or help – not gnash your teeth and curse the cost of calling in some trumped-up expert who came, saw and delivered an account for remote services rendered.

A Swiss management consultancy firm included this 'light relief' item at the end of one of its annual reports: 'When the consultants first came in I was confused; when they left I was still confused, but at a far higher level.'

Summary

- Consultants provide second opinions as well as solutions.

- Consultants or other 'outside' advisers can bring a fresh mind to problem-solving. They are not caught up in the day-to-day running of your business, nor are they involved with company politics. They can often act as an ideal catalyst or, because of their independence, 'defuse' tricky situations.

- Ensure you define or outline problems thoroughly. Supply and share information; display trust.

- Ascertain ground rules regarding progress reporting, charging, timing and so on at the outset.

- Empathy – ask yourself 'How well can we work with this person/these people?'

- Talk to advisers' clients or neutral referral sources. Do not accept advisers' claims without checking.

- Be wary of advisers who initially appear as a committee. In the final analysis, it generally boils down to a one-to-one relationship.

- Remember, we all make mistakes. Watch it if your advisers claim to 'know it all' or display a tendency to always be in the right. Success comes through a sound, flexible, trusting, two-way working relationship.

28

The chief executive and marketing

The chief executive is critical to the creation of a marketing orientation in any organisation, and nowhere is this better illustrated than in the experience of British companies.

The prime role of any chief executive is to establish the culture, strategy, priorities and organisation necessary for his company to make most effective use of its assets, within the context of the particular business environment in which it is operating.

The overall business environment has changed dramatically over the past century, and particularly in the forty years since the Second World War. Some two hundred years ago Britain was in the vanguard of the industrial revolution, with emphasis on technological and manufacturing development to produce an ever increasing volume of products to meet the demand from the new personal and industrial consumers in both the UK and what was essentially a captive empire market.

Greater production output was the order of the day and continued through until the recession of the late 1920s and early 1930s. Then, before any major reorientation of business thinking was implemented, the demands and destruction of the last war left the UK and much of the industrialised world in a chronic undersupply situation, with emphasis once more on the need for manufacturing output to meet the post war shortages and pent-up demand.

During the last thirty years, considerable change of emphasis has taken place, with the spotlight and orientation of management moving from manufacturing through finance, taxation, selling and industrial relations, to the cost cutting and labour shedding, rationalisation period of the late 1970s and early 1980s, as companies strove to survive, and combat increasingly successful international competitors.

Also in the period since the war, many British companies, even entire industries, have been decimated as very aggressive foreign competitors met the needs of much more discriminating customers with better quality, higher added value products and services, supported by well thought through market strategies and service operations.

These pressures increased as the world recession began to bite at the end of the 1970s, with most companies concentrating their survival efforts on improved manufacturing efficiency, increased productivity, cost cutting and reduced manning levels to achieve a welcome improvement in profitability, and become more cost competitive than they had been for years.

However, only a minority of British companies like ICI, Jaguar and BA translated these improvements into market place advantage and competed aggressively in the international arena. Most did not and have not increased sales volume or market share. Now, in many cases, with rising costs, particularly labour, and little real scope for further productivity and cost reduction gains, profits are beginning to level off and decline. Rationalisation proposals are back again on board agendas.

The fact that so many UK companies have either not been aware of the need to adapt to the changed market environment, or have not been capable of adapting to it, has to be an indictment of the understanding and competence of the chief executives concerned. It is not therefore a surprise that surveys show them to be singularly low in their level of formal business training, and that many have no major marketing or sales experience. Because of our history over the last two centuries, there is also a lack of competitive culture in the UK compared with Japan, USA and West Germany, where they have not had the benefit of the British educational and social attitudes.

Indeed recent research showed that many British companies admit they are not good at marketing, do not have clearly defined market strategies and objectives, and do not use basic marketing disciplines like market research, new product design and development or consultancy. It is perhaps fortunate, although sad, that the lack of any other major route to profit improvement, has now concentrated the minds of many chief executives on their market place and how to exploit it, probably for the first time.

Increasingly they are seeking and responding to the assistance that is available, to enhance their personal understanding of the critical influence of marketing on their business and to develop the marketing strategies necessary to adapt to and exploit their particular market environment.

These shortcomings are not exclusive to any type or size of organisation, although they are most prevalent in the industrial products sector and in small firms generally. Companies in manufactured consumer goods, retailing and services, appear to have adapted more successfully, although this is by no means general even in these sectors.

It is also significant that research indicates the most consistently successful companies are market driven, and are led by chief executives with a strong personal conviction about the critical importance of the market place.

These are not surprising findings, since the ultimate success or failure of a company must depend on customers choosing to purchase that firm's products or services in preference to those of a competitor. Orientating the company towards meeting the changed needs of customers and providing something better than competitors, is fundamental to any business, but it will only happen if the chief executive stimulates such a commitment throughout the company.

Being marketing oriented does not mean having a marketing department. It is an attitude of mind which accepts that there is no business until a customer buys and therefore the whole orientation of the company has to be towards achieving this. Many companies do not have a specific marketing department, the whole organisation is it. Indeed, a strong marketing department can sometimes mean that the rest of the organisation feels it does not need to be concerned.

But, whatever the structure, the critical influence on whether the company is or is not market orientated, has to be the chief executive. He sets the culture, defines the strategy and drives the business.

British chief executives tend to be heavily single-disciple rather than rounded businessmen, and have arrived in the position because the company needed a particular skill at a particular time in its development. During the last forty years, these particular skill needs varied as we have seen, but what was ignored in the UK was the overriding influence of a changing international market place and increasingly aggressive competitors.

When Ted Levitt demonstrated corporate shortsightedness to its changing market environment, in *Marketing Myopia* over twenty years ago, he assumed that companies were at least looking at their market place, albeit in a blinkered way.

Unfortunately, in the UK even this was not the case; many British companies were only looking at individual elements of the business and often the chief executive had little if any real interest or direct involvement in the market place or with its customers.

With a generation of business school trained chief executives now coming through, and a decade of intense competition throwing up entrepreneurs who can handle it, the situation in UK companies is changing quickly and dramatically. However, there are still thousands of companies with chief executives who do not understand marketing thinking and are not comfortable in a customer environment. To overcome this, many initiatives have been taken by government, professional bodies and companies, to provide marketing briefings, workshops, counselling and consultancy.

The response from chief executives to these initiatives has been very positive as has their reaction to the content of them. One can only wonder why they have not acted sooner.

In the recently published *Marketing Edge*, which distilled the critical factors for any company to be successful in a competitive market environment, the orientation and commitment of the chief executive was shown as one of the most important.

British companies have arrived via a very tortuous route, at the basic business truth which Adam Smith emphasised two centuries ago in the *Wealth of Nations*, that the market place determines whether or not a company is successful. What he could have added was that chief executives determine whether or not their company will act on that basic business truth, to take full advantage of the international market opportunities which are now opening up.

Never has the chief executive's involvement in marketing been more crucial to the company's prosperity.

Summary

The chief executive is central to a company's marketing orientation. What is essential is the attitude of mind, not a particular background or training. It is necessary in any business – consumer, service or industrial.

29
Where do we go from here?

The very essence of business is to find and convince customers that it is better for them to buy your product or service, than the ones your competitors are offering. Over the decades other business considerations have appeared to be more important than customers, but sooner or later companies with these beliefs have had to change, or they ran into trouble.

For limited periods there have been crises in manufacturing, labour relations, finance, quality, management; but underlying everything, there is the truism that until the customer buys, there are only costs and there is no business.

As the other critical elements in any company are organised effectively, and as international competition increases in a market environment that is changing at an even faster rate, Darwin's theory of adapt to the changing environment or perish, rings increasingly true.

Change is taking place everywhere – economic, social, technological, cultural, demographic, financial; in communication, distribution, in the type and intensity of competition, and in the expectations and sophistication of consumers.

Take any industry, business or market and you can see the implications of change, and the price companies have paid when they failed to recognise and adapt their strategies and organisations to the market and customer change.

Thus it follows that chief executives must appreciate and understand the role of marketing and its impact on the total business operation.

Effective marketing thinking and disciplines will not by themselves make a company successful; the other parts of the business must also be operating well. But one thing is certain, if marketing is not effective the company will not survive in a competitive environment, no matter how well the rest of the business is managed.

Marketing in the round

The marketing we describe is a way of running a business and using its assets to best advantage, and it starts with the chief executive and permeates company thinking and operations.

We are not talking simply about marketing tactics, tools or departments, important as they are. Nor do we question the impact of a very persuasive advertising campaign, or well-trained, well-motivated sales people; or the appeal of a stylishly designed and appealingly packaged new product; or the clever and creative interpretation of some perceptive consumer or market research.

We are talking about the total orientation of the business and how its strategy and organisation is matched to the market and competitive environment in which it is operating.

This is the essential reality of marketing, and the most effective tactics and tools to use – and the best mix of them – can only be determined when the strategy is formulated and the organisation is capable of implementing it.

Future trends

The only certain thing about the future is that it will change, and the change will be greater and faster than we have experienced over the last few decades. Take the trouble to look back ten and twenty years at lifestyles, technology, fashion, music, social attitudes, governments, travel, environmental turbulence, retailing, energy, personal expectations. Then project forward even that same rate of change, and you will have an indication of the dramatically different environment in which you will be operating, and the implications on your business.

But whatever the change, there will always be customers, there will always be competitors, and there will always be opportunities to build successful, profitable businesses by finding and satisfying the former and beating the latter.

That is what marketing is all about.